SEVEN LITTLE AUSTRALIANS

Based on the classic novel by
ETHEL TURNER

Adapted by
DAVID REEVES

Includes some material from the David Reeves film script (2007) and the book/lyrics of the 1988 musical by Peter Yeldham, John Palmer and David Reeves.

ORiGiN™
Theatrical

FOR ALL ENQUIRIES CONTACT: ORiGiN™ Theatrical
PO BOX Q1235, QVB Post Office, Sydney, NSW, 1230, Australia
Phone: (61 2) 8514 5201 Fax: (61 2) 9299 2920
enquiries@originmusic.com.au   www.origintheatrical.com.au
Part of the ORiGiN™ Music Group
An Australian Independent Music Company

1

Cover Photo
Thanks to
Stage Right Youth Theatre, Launceston
Photographer Brian Dullaghan

IMPORTANT NOTICE

should not be considered to be necessarily endorsing or otherwise attempting to promote an affiliation with any of the owners of the brand names or trademarks or public figures. Such references are solely for use in a dramatic context.

LANGUAGE NOTE

Licensees are welcome to make small alterations to the language that is used is this play so as to make it suitable for a younger cast and/or audience.

MUSIC USE NOTE

Licensees are solely responsible for obtaining formal written permission from copyright owners to use copyrighted music in the performance of this play and are strongly cautioned to do so. If no such permission is obtained by the licensee, then the licensee must use only original music that the licensee owns and controls. Licensees are solely responsible and liable for all music clearances and shall indemnify the copyright owners of the play(s) and their licensing agent, ORiGiN™ Theatrical, against any costs, expenses, losses and liabilities arising from the use of music by licensees. Please contact the appropriate music licensing authority in your territory for the rights to any incidental music. In Australia and New Zealand, contact APRA AMCOS apraamcos.com.au.

If you are in any doubt about any of the above then contact ORiGiN™ Theatrical.

For complete listing of plays and musicals available to perform and all licence enquiries, contact ORiGiN™ Theatrical.

www.origintheatrical.com.au
+ 61 2 8514 5201

AND HERE ARE THE RULES
IN PLAIN ENGLISH FOR YOU...

<u>DO NOT</u> perform this play without getting permission from ORiGiN™ Theatrical first. In 99% of cases you'll need to pay us money to be allowed to stage a performance. This money goes to the author(s) of the show who shed blood, sweat and tears creating this play. Please don't rob them of their livelihood.
Go online www.origintheatrical.com.au or call +61 2 8514 5201

<u>DO NOT</u> make a copy of this book by photocopying, scanning, taking a photo, retyping (on a computer or a typewriter), or using a pencil, pen or chalkboard. If you want to purchase more copies contact ORiGiN™ Theatrical.
Go online www.origintheatrical.com.au or call +61 2 8514 5201

<u>DO NOT</u> make any changes to the text without first getting permission from ORiGiN™ Theatrical in writing. Sometimes you'll be allowed to make changes and sometimes you won't. Please always check with us first.
Go online www.origintheatrical.com.au or call +61 2 8514 5201

<u>DO NOT</u> record your performances or rehearsals in anyway without first getting permission from ORiGiN™ Theatrical. We know everyone wants to try and record everything on their phones these days. We get it. But please don't encourage them or give them permission. Sometimes there are important contractual reasons as to why we can't give you permission to record it. And sometimes there aren't any reasons and we can say YES. Please just check with us first.
Go online www.origintheatrical.com.au or call +61 2 8514 5201

<u>DO</u> contact ORiGiN™ Theatrical if you have any questions about anything. At all. And we mean anything. One of us that works here (not me) has a peculiar interest in recording the unusual bird calls of the adult hoatzin (a species of tropical bird found in wet forest and mangrove of the Amazon and the Orinoco delta in South America) so we should be able to answer any questions you have about the Hoatzin. Plus we know some things about some other things too.

Thank you for taking the time to read this.

BY THE SAME AUTHOR

7 Little Australians (the musical)

Cyrano de Bergerac (the musical)

Stage Door Songbook - Songs from Australian musicals

AUTHOR - DAVID REEVES

Australian expatriate Australian composer, organist, and conductor, David Reeves was born in Sydney, Australia in 1943. His first professional organ post was as Director of Music at the 'Garrison Church' at the Rocks whilst still at school. He studied at the Sydney Conservatorium of Music under Alexander Sverjensky(piano) and George Faunce Allman and Norman Johnston (organ). He won both ofthe coveted overseas music scholarships available in the early sixties, the Alice Bryant Memorial Scholarship for Organists and the Sydney Organ Society Scholarship for Overseas Study.

After returning to Australia from London he was appointed Director of Music at Abbotsleigh by Betty Archdale where he remained based for three years building the music department whilst at the same time arranging and performing. He worked as a recitalist in all the main venues in Australia including radio broadcasts by the A.B.C. He was especially sought after for his final improvisations which concluded nearly all his recitals and were a feature of his liturgical performance. He became particularly identified with the famous 'Hill' organ in the Sydney Town Hall where he worked extensively between 1963 and 1978 as a recitalist and performing at Civic Receptions, School Speech Days, even evenings for the presentation of advertising awards and in broadcasts for the A.B.C. as well as annual performances of both the Bach St. Matthew and St. John passions. He recorded the first commercial organ alburm on the Unison label in 1971 which set a record for sales of organ recordings at the time. Over the next six years he went on to record nine organ albums on instruments throughout the country.

He accompanied the very popular annual Combined Churches' presentations of Handel's "Messiah" conducted by Richard Thew for eighteen years. These performances filled The Sydney Town Hall for three nights each year and were a highlight of the Christmas calendar in the sixties and eventies. During this period he was appointed accompanist for the Sydney University Graduate Choir whose choral repertoire was wide and included the major works of Bach and the Baroque composers. He held several church positions as Organist and Director of Music, the first of which was at the Garrison Church in Sydney's Rocks area whilst still at school.

The renowned firm of English organ builders, J.W. Walker and Sons expanded into Australia in the 1960's and appointed Reeves as their recitalist leading to the opening recitals of many new and rebuilt organs throughout Australia. He also indulged is passion for jazz at several venues in Sydney and for several months took on the musical direction of a leading Sydney nightclub until his other commitments made this impossible.

In the late seventies he started to move more into advertising, film and commercial music and was awarded many creative contracts including the Hanna Barbera Christmas film of "Silent Night", the musical recording "Pilgrimage" a commercial album celebrating the musical highlights of the first Papal Tour of Australia, a music and poetry album featuring the voice and writing of Sydney radio personality John Laws. During this time he was a regular adjudicator for Channel Nine in Sydney with its 'New Faces' Talent Programmes.

Music education has always been a passion and Reeves has adjudicated numerous Eisteddfods including the City of Sydney, Parramatta, Gunnedah and Tamworth Eisteddfods amongst many others. He has given workshops, been appointed as 'composer in residence' including at Gordonstoun School in Scotland, and was the founder of the Australian "Operation Young Composer" Award programme which has provided opportunity for overseas study for several young Australian composers, including Neridah Tyson.

The Australian Bicentennial Authority appointed Reeves as composer for the soundtrack to the promotional film for the "Tall Ships" celebration on Sydney Harbour in 1988. Also in that year his theatre musical, _Seven Little Australians_ based on the classic Australian story originally created by Ethel Turner, opened at the Comedy Theatre in Melbourne. The musical was to run for two hundred and thirty performances in the main theatres throughout the eastern states. The Royal Queensland Theatre Company produced a sellout season in 1991 and David Reeves was nominated for an ARIA award for his score and original EMI cast recording of _Seven Little Australians_. The amateur rights are now regularly taken up and many musical societies have performed the piece in recent years. The musical is currently being adapted for film.

8

David Reeves' opera *Cyrano de Bergerac* was similarly received when recorded by members of the Queensland Opera accompanied by the Queensland Symphony Orchestra. Concert performances of the opera were given in 1995 under the auspices of the Queensland Performing Arts Trust and the opera was narrated by Sir John Mills. Reeves was presented with the Variety Club Award for Service to the Arts in 1995.

By now completely based in London, he scored Oscar Wilde's *The Picture of Dorian Gray* which was performed on the West End. The treatment of the text was extremely controversial which was reflected in several negative critiques in 1997. In 1999 Reeves returned to more conventional texts and recorded his oratorio *Becket-The Kiss of Peace*.

A subsequent performance of this work became the highlight of the Canterbury Festival in 2000. The performance was given under the auspices of HRH Prince Charles and raised funds for the Prince's Trust. The performance featured the choristers of Canterbury Cathedral with the English Chamber Singers, the English Festival Orchestra and soloists including James Bowman, Gillian Keith and David Wilson Johnson. In the critiques Sir David Willcocks wrote as follows: "In the 'Kiss of Peace' the gifted Australian composer, David Reeves has produced a score that judging by the response of the singers and indeed all who heard it when first performed, gave great pleasure and was truly enjoyed. It is a work that appeals to all. Reeves is not afraid to write music that is truly approachable, beautiful and memorable."

Amongst Reeves' many recordings a recent EP release is one featuring highlights from recordings made at Canterbury Cathedral, including a performance of Reeves' *"Tuba Tune"* performed by the composer.

David Reeves has recently been commissioned to write a work on the subject of St. Francis of Assisi by the organisers of the Assisi Festival of Peace. The work "*Planet Requiem*" is to be a feature of the Festival in 2008 and is to be performed in the Franciscan Basilica in Assisi Italy, under the baton of the composer.

The musical "*James and Maggie*" based on the story of J C Williamson the Australian theatrical impresario was highlighted at the Oz Musicals 2006 in Melbourne Australia. It was written with Peter Yeldham in 1991.

He is currently in Australia developing a musical feature film based on *Seven Little Australians* as a joint venture between the UK and Australia.

10

THE SCENES

ACT ONE

SCENE 1   'YARRAHAPPINI' - THE WOOLSHED - TWILIGHT

SCENE 2   'MISRULE' – INTERIOR - EARLY EVENING

SCENE 3   WOOLCOT'S STUDY – EARLY MORNING

SCENE 4   ON THE TRAM

SCENE 5   THE PARADE GROUND – VICTORIA BARRACKS

SCENE 6   BACK ON THE TRAM – LATE AFTERNOON

SCENE 7   WOOLCOT'S STUDY - SATURDAY NIGHT

SCENE 8   'MISRULE' INTERIOR SCENE - EARLY MORNING

SCENE 9   BARE STAGE – LIGHTS DIMMED

SCENE 10   MISS BURTON'S ACADEMY FOR GIRLS IN THE BLUE
           MOUNTAINS

SCENE 11   'MISRULE' – INTERIOR – EARLY MORNING

ACT TWO

SCENE 1   'MISRULE' – INTERIOR - EVENING

SCENE 2   WOOLCOT'S STUDY – ONE WEEK LATER – MORNING

SCENE 3   DARKNESS – THE NIGHT RIDER

SCENE 4   WOOLCOT'S STUDY – EVENING

SCENE 5   WOOLCOT'S STUDY - DAY

SCENE 6   YARRAHAPPINI RAILWAY STATION – SUNRISE

SCENE 7   'YARRAHAPPINI STATION' MORNING

SCENE 8   WOOLCOT'S STUDY – MORNING

SCENE 9   THE WOOLSHED AT YARRAHAPPINI – TWILIGHT

SCENE 10   DARKNESS – THE BARE STAGE

SCENE 11   'YARRAHAPPINI' – THE WOOLSHED – ONE YEAR LATER
           - TWILIGHT

CHARACTERS

CAPTAIN WOOLCOT LATE FOURTIES. A RESOLUTE AND GOOD MAN, WELL BRED WHO STRUGGLES IN HIS NEW CIRCUMSTANCES. HE ACTS WITH BRAVADO BUT IS A INSECURE. HE IS THE VILLAIN IN THE STORY FOR ALL OF ACT ONE BUT DURING ACT TWO HE STANDS UP TO HIS COMMANDING OFFICER AND IN THE PROCESS FINDS HIS TRUE RELATIONSHIP WITH HIS WIFE AND HIS CHILDREN, ESPECIALLY JUDY.

ESTHER WOOLCOT BEAUTIFUL, RADIANT AND INNOCENT SECOND WIFE OF CAPTAIN WOOLCOT. IN HER EARLY TWENTIES AND WHILE VERY YOUNG, GROWS THROUGH THE SHOW, PROVING TO BE STRONG AND SOMETIMES FEISTY.

COLONEL BRYANT POMPOUS AND ARROGANT. VERY SUPERIOR AND DEMEANING TO THOSE BENEATH HIM WHETHER IN THE MILITARY OR THE PUBLIC. HE AND MRS BRYANT ARE FORMIDABLE, SUPERIOR COUPLE.

MRS BRYANT THE WIFE OF COLONEL BRYANT. SIMLIARLY SUPERIOR AND SPEAKS WITH A SMELL UNDER HER NOSE.

MARTHA IRISH HOUSEKEEPER WITH OPINIONS OF HER OWN AND HER OWN SENSE OF HUMOUR. SAFE IN THE KNOWLEDGE NO-ONE ELSE WOULD TAKE HER JOB OR WORK FOR THE MONEY THE WOOLCOTS CAN AFFORD TO PAY HER. SHE TAKES CERTAIN LIBERTIES BUT LOVES THEM ALL.

ALAN COURTNEY THE YOUNG DOCTOR, JUST COMPLETING MEDICINE.

12

MISS BURTON	A STERN SPINSTER HEADMISTRESS WITH VERY VICTORIAN VIEWS ABOUT POLITE SOCIETY.
ALDITH McCARTHY	A LOUD, BRASCH TEENAGER WHO COMMANDS ATTENTION AND WHO POSSESSES A UNIQUE, PENETRATING VOICE.
DR GORMISTON	A MIDDLE AGED, PORTLY COUNTRY DOCTOR. A MAN OF THE PERIOD, VERY PROPER AND A PILLAR OF COMMUNITY.
MR HASSAL	A WEALTHY WEATHERED SUCCESSFUL GRAZIER IN HIS EARLY SEVENTIES WITH A GAMY LEG...
MRS HASSAL	MR HASSAL'S TINY FUSSED AND BUSY WIFE WHO IS NO-ONE'S FOOL AND LOVES HER GRANDCHILDREN.
MR GILLET	A GAUNT AND REFINED OLDER LOOKING MAN FROM THE OLD COUNTRY, RESPLENDENT WITH A TRIMMED WHITE BEARD.
TRAM CONDUCTOR	A NEW AUSTRALIAN STRUGGLING WITH THE LANGUAGE.
TETTAWONGA	AN OLD ABORIGINAL WHO HAS LIVED ON THE YARRAHAPPINI PROPERTY SINCE THE ARRIVAL OF THE HASSALS.
MISS JOLLY	AN ELDERLY SPINSTER TEACHER, EMPLOYED BY MISS BURTON FOR MANY YEARS. SHE PEERS MYOPICALLY THROUGH A PINCE-NEZ.

THE CHILDREN
JUDY, NELL, MEG, BUNTY, PIP, BABY, THE LITTLE GENERAL

ADDITIONAL SMALL PARTS PLAYED BY LADIES/GENTLEMEN OF THE CHORUS

ANDREW COURTNEY

ALAN COURTNEY'S BROTHER

FARMHAND 1

FARMHAND 2

THE HORSES (TWO/FOUR STAGEHANDS)

BEATRICE

JANET

GROOMSMAN/DOGCART DRIVER

HEARSE DRIVER

YARRAHAPPINI KITCHEN HAND

BLUE

THE SQUATTER

POLICE SERGEANT

POLICE CONSTABLE

CORPORAL

SENTRY

FIVE SOLDIERS OF THE REGIMENT

THREE MALE TRAVELLERS ON THE TRAM

ELDERLY LADY TRAM PASSENGER

AND

LADIES AND GENTLEMEN

THE DESIGN

*SET DESIGN SHOULD CONSIDER THE REQUIREMENT FOR SLICK, SILENT AND VERY EFFICIENT QUICK SET CHANGE REQUIREMENTS.

*THE DESIGN SUGGESTED IN THIS ADAPTION REPRESENTS A SUGGESTION ONLY. IT IS ONE OF SEVERAL OPTIONS, THE FIRST OF WHICH CENTRES AROUND A REVOLVE AND A TURNING 'MISRULE' THAT HIGHLIGHTS AN EXTERIOR AND (ON TURNING) AN INTERIOR WITH VARIOUS CAMEO POSSIBILITIES IN BETWEEN. THE SECOND USES LED LIGHTING (AND OTHER EMERGING TECHNOLOGIES) WHICH CAN MERGE EXTERIOR WITH INTERIOR VERY SUCCESFULLY. THAT IS NOT TO MENTION THE POSSIBILITIES WITH REGARD TO THE RIVER/FRONT GARDEN/ VARIOUS IMAGES WITHIN 'YARRAHAPPINI'.

IN FACT THERE ARE MANY COMBINATIONS WITHIN TRADITIONAL DESIGN AND THE NEW TECHNOLOGIES. I ENCOURAGE NEW IDEAS IN NEW PRODUCTIONS THAT I HOPE WILL BE PRODUCED IN THE FUTURE.

David Reeves – SYDNEY 2018

THE SETS

THE 'MISRULE' INTERIOR

'MISRULE' - INTERIOR SET. A FOYER/HALLWAY SITS AT THE FOOT OF A TIRED BUT GRAND STAIRCASE LEADING TO A DRESS CIRCLE SECOND FLOOR WALKWAY ABOVE. THE MASTER BEDROOM DOORWAY IS THE ONLY DOOR OFF THE PROMPT SIDE OF THE UPSTAIRS WALK-WAY WHILST THERE ARE THREE DOORS [MEG, JUDY/NELL/BABY AND PIP/BUNTY] AT THE OFF PROMPT SIDE. AT GROUND LEVEL ARE DOORS TO THE DINING ROOM [PROMPT], TO THE NURSERY [OFF PROMPT], WITH A SWING DOOR TO THE KITCHEN AREA. A FURTHER DOORWAY ACCESSES THE REAR OF THE HOUSE. NEAR THE DINING ROOM DOORWAY SITS A SMALL VICTORIAN DESK, A HALL STAND NEARBY, AND SEVERAL SHELVES FEATURE ON A WALL. THERE IS AN IMAGINARY FRONT DOOR THAT SQUEAKS AND GROANS. IT IS APPROACHED BY STAIRS LEADING UP TO A DOORSTEP FROM WHERE AN ORCHESTRA PIT WOULD TRADITIONALLY BE. TWO SHORT QUARTER WIDTH STAGE EXTENSIONS FLANK THE STAGE FRONT AT PROMPT AND OFF PROMPT.

THE SET IS IN FOUR PARTS:

1) An elaborate but tired staircase reaching three quarter stage height built on a movable truck with position lockable wheels.

2) An upstairs dress-circle walkway with opening doors is lowered from the grid.

3) An off-prompt 'side' set containing the Nursery [that spills out onto the off-prompt stage flank] and the cladding that flows from its access through to the back of the staircase.

4) A prompt 'side' set containing the Dining room [that spills out onto the prompt stage flank] and the cladding that flows from its access trough to the back of the staircase.

'WOOLCOT'S STUDY'

A PARTNER'S DESK LOOKS OUT THROUGH OPEN FRENCH WINDOWS TO THE VERANDAH, THE ROSEBUSH, AND IN THE DISTANCE THE WILLOW, AND THE RIVER BEYOND. A WALL OF

16

BOOKSHELVES, AN UPRIGHT PIANO AND OCCASIONAL CHAIRS
MAKE UP THE FURNITURE.

THE TRAM

AN EARLY SYDNEY 'TOAST RACK' ELECTRIC TRAM. IT IS SET AT
AN ANGLE TO THE AUDIENCE TO PROVIDE THE BEST SIGHTLINE
TO THE KEY PASSENGERS. SEATING IS ARRANGED BETWEEN
SEVERAL DUET SETS OF FACING BENCHES AS EXISTED AT THE
TIME, MOUNTED HIGH ON RISERS. A CONDUCTOR PRANCES
ALONG THE LENGTH OF THE TRAM ON A 'FOOT BOARD' [RUNNING
BOARD THAT KEEPS ALL HEADS ABOUT THE SAME HEIGHT]
STAGE FRONT. THE ROOF AND BRASS RAILS [WHICH THE
CONDUCTOR HOLDS AND FROM WHICH HE HANGS OFF THE
TRAM] FORM PART OF THE PHYSICAL TRAM UNIT 'TRUCK' THAT
MOVES ON WHEELS.

THE TRAM SITS FIXED, FOR THE MOST PART. IT SITS BEFORE A
MOVING PROJECTION WHOSE IMAGES COVER THE SCENIC
JOURNEY FROM CIRCULAR QUAY, INTO BRIDGE STREET, THENCE
INTO ELIZABETH, TURNING INTO WILLIAM, JOINING OXFORD
STREET TOWARDS VICTORIA BARRACKS, THE TRAMSHEDS AT
THE JUNCTION, THENCE DOWN BONDI ROAD TO BONDI BEACH.

A TRAM SHELTER WITH A LONG BENCH RESTS ON THE FOOTPATH
IN FRONT OF BACK CLOTH. IT IS WALLED ON THREE SIDES AND
TRUCKS ON AND OFF, ONLY BECOMING VISIBLE TO AUDIENCE
WHEN THE TRAM TRUCKS OFF.

PROJECTIONS INCLUDE:

1) A strip of joined art drawings/paintings covering highlights of the journey
between the Circular Quay Terminal and the Bondi Beach 'Loop'. [For use as
a 'forward' projection and 'reverse']

2) A strip of joined art drawings/paintings covering highlights of the journey
between the Yarrahappini Railway Station and the Yarrahappini Sheep Station
and Homestead.

3) A strip of joined art drawings/paintings covering the buildings and features
covered in Scene 7 – ACT TWO.

4) A single rear projection depicting sandstone buildings, cottages, out -

houses, the homestead in the distance, the woolshed with its trees and billabong nearby, paddocks and holding pens etc. repeats of the projection shows the morning sun at three different stages in the sky.

'THE YARRAHAPPINI WOOLSHED'

A WOOLSHED INTERIOR THAT LOOKS BACK THROUGH A HUGE OPEN DOUBLE DOOR ENTRANCE PITCHED AT 45 DEGREES ON OFF PROMPT BETWEEN A POINT ONE THIRD OF THE WAY IN SETTING LINE TOWARD BACK STAGE. THROUGH THE DOORS WE SEE THE HOMESTEAD IN THE DISTANCE, THE MANY TREES BETWEEN, ONE LARGE AND PROMINENT WITH A BILLABONG NEARBY.

****

"Be careful of Judy. Don't let her become shipwrecked on rocks that the others would never come to"
- Ethel Turner

THE PLAY

ACT ONE

ACT ONE   SCENE 1

'YARRAHAPPINI' - THE WOOLSHED – TWILIGHT.

A SIGN ILLUMINATES IN THE CENTRE OF THE PROSCENIUM ARCH. [ALL SIGNS ARE WRITTEN IN THE STYLE OF 'RONALD SEARLE' – 'DOWN WITH SKOOL'] IT READS: 'YARRAHAPPINI'.

TWO SHORT QUARTER WIDTH STAGE EXTENTIONS PROTRUDE INTO THE AUDITORIOUM AT BOTH SIDES.

A WEDDING IS TAKING PLACE IN FRONT OF A BACKING CLOTH SET A QUARTER WAY BACK FROM THE SETTING LINE. PROJECTED ON TO THE CLOTH IS WOOLSHED INTERIOR. LOOKING BACK THROUGH HUGE OPEN DOUBLE DOORS CAN BE SEEN THE MAGNIFICENT HOMESTEAD IN THE DISTANCE, THE MANY TREES CLOSER IN, ONE LARGE AND PROMINENT NEAR A LARGE BILLABONG.

AT FRONT ARE ASSEMBLED THE GUESTS IN BRIGHTLY COLOURED COSTUMES SPILL ONTO THE STAGE WHICH IS DECKED IN BRIGHT FLOWERS AND WEDDING DECOR.

A WEDDING PARTY STANDS AT A FORTY- FIVE DEGREE ANGLE TO THE SETTING LINE BEAUTIFUL, RADIANT, TWENTY ONE YEAR OLD BRIDE, ESTHER HASSAL IS FLANKED BY BRIDESMAIDS MEG, JUDY AND NELL. BABY IS A FLOWER GIRL HOLDING THE END OF ESTHER'S TRAIN BEHIND. ON ESTHER'S OTHER SIDE

23

STANDS JOHN WOOLCOT, FLANKED BY
GROOMSMEN PIP AND BUNTY. BRIDE AND
GROOM FACE A RUDDY FACED, JOVIAL VICAR.
BEHIND THE BRIDAL PARTY STANDS THE WELL
WEATHERED MR HASSAL, A WEALTHY COUNTRY
SQUIRE WITH AKUBRA HAT, MRS HASSAL
STANDING AT THE HEAD OF THE GUESTS, JUST
BEHIND. COLONEL BRYANT, IN FULL MILITARY
DRESS WITH MEDALS, AND MRS BRYANT ARE
PROMINENT GUESTS, AS ARE MR GILLET AND
TETTAWONGA.

AT RISE:

THE PROJECTION SHOWS THE LATE AFTERNOON
SUN RETREATING. THE SERVICE IS IN PROGRESS.

VICAR:
For as much as John and... (A JOVIAL LOVING SMILE,
AS HE LOOKS AT HER) ... Esther ...

(THE INNOCENT ESTHER TURNS ADORINGLY
TOWARDS HER MAN)

VICAR:
.... have consented together in holy wedlock ...

(A COUGH IS HEARD FROM MR GILLET AMONG
THE GUESTS)

VICAR:
(TO ESTHER) Do you take this man to be your wedded
husband, to have and to hold, from this day forward, for
better, for worse, (EXAGGERATING) for richer,
(LOWERING VOICE) for poorer.

(SFX SQUAWKING BIRDS - A LONG LINE OF
GALAHS SITS PERCHED ON A BEAM INSIDE THE
WOOLSHED.

WE BECOME FURTHER AWARE OF THE POMPOUS
COLONEL BRYANT, AND MRS BRYANT, A VERY
SUPERIOR LOOKING COUPLE)

BRYANT:
(TO HIS WIFE) Too OLD, I say.

(WE BECOME AWARE OF TETTAWONGA DRESSED
IN A 'DOWN AND OUT' STYLE BAGGY RAGGED
OLD SUIT, COLOURED SHIRT AND TIE. HE STANDS
NEXT TO MR GILLET, DRESSED IN TAILS AND
HOLDING A TOP HAT)

MR GILLET:
(TO TETTAWONGA) …and SIX children!

VICAR:
(OMINOUSLY).... 'til death do you part?

ESTHER:
(EXCITEDLY) I certainly do.

(A CHUCKLE RISES FROM THE GUESTS)

(THE SERVICE PROCEEDS UNHEARD BY THE
AUDIENCE)

BRYANT:
(STERNLY TO MRS BRYANT) An unruly tribe! No
discipline since the first Mrs Woolcot's passing!

MRS BRYANT:

(STUDIES THE WEDDING PARTY. TURNS BACK TO
BRYANT AND SPEAKS AS IF THERE IS A SMELL
UNDER HER NOSE) Which is which?

BRYANT:

From memory... the eldest is Margaret, better known as
Meg. She appears to be the maid of honour, no less.

(MEG IS COMELY AND BEAUTIFUL AS THE FIRST
BRIDESMAID. SHE SMOOTHS DOWN ESTHER'S
TRAIN ON WHICH AN UNCOORDINATED PIP IS
APPARENTLY STANDING, WITH BABY TRYING TO
GET HIM OFF)

BABY:

Git Oth, Pip!

BRYANT:

(POINTING RUDELY) Over there.... Pip. First son, and
heir. He seems to be best man.

MRS BRYANT:

(NOTICING NELL) Oh... and I remember little Nell, the
flower girl.... nearest to Woolcot. Always so angelic.

BRYANT:

(GESTURING TOWARDS BUNTY) And you wouldn't
have forgotten Bunty... that lazy, fat, good for nothing...

(BUNTY THE SECOND GROOMSMAN LOOKS
BORED AND SLOVENLY)

MRS BRYANT:

Oh, you don't MEAN that?

BRYANT:
I DO! …the lazy, fat…

MRS BRYANT:
(CUTTING HIM OFF AND GESTURING TO BABY) I suppose the other flower girl is the baby of the family. I don't think we've met her, have we?

BRYANT:
But we have … at the CHRISTENING! Remember?

MRS BRYANT:
Of course. How silly of me. Someone knocked over the alter candle… and nearly burnt down the church.

BRYANT:
THAT was the time!

MRS BRYANT:
Oooh, yes. Who was that WILD one? Where is SHE in that lot?

BRYANT:
Ah… yes. Judy. 'Trouble'… I call her.

(WE BECOME AWARE OF JUDY WHO IS TRYING TO TICKLE THE DOCILE BUT PERPLEXED FLOWER-GIRL NELL, THEN WITHDRAWING QUICKLY AWAY SO AS NOT TO BE NOTICED)

VICAR:
(RESUMING PROMINENCE AND OVER-RIDING THE OTHERS) I declare....

(THE VICAR IS ELATED, SMILING WITH
AUTHORITY AS ALL ATTENTION TURNS BACK TO
HIM)

VICAR:

.... John and Esther…man and wife. For those whom God
has joined together, let no man put asunder!

(THE GATHERING APPLAUDS AS THE VICAR
LEADS THE BRIDAL COUPLE TOWARD A TABLE
SET AT OFF PROMPT ON WHICH RESTS A LARGE
VOLUME RESTING REGALLY ON A LECTERN
AWAITING SIGNATURES THAT WILL REGISTER
THE MARRIAGE.

MRS HASSAL, LOOKING FUSSED AND BUSY, NOW
JOINS THE WEDDING PARTY AS MR HASSAL
AFFECTIONATELY PECKS HIS TINY WIFE ON THE
CHEEK)

TETTAWONGA:

(TO MR GILLET) Won't be the same roun' 'ere …

MR GILLET:

(LOOKING TOWARD MR HASSAL) I wonder what her
daddy really thinks?

(SUDDENLY THERE IS A LOUD CRACK OF
THUNDER. ALL LOOK TO OUTSIDE WHERE THE
SKY HAS TURNED DARK, BLOCKING THE SUN.
TETTAWONGA STARTS TO BLOW INTO HIS
DIDGERIDOO.

THE LADIES HOLD DOWN THEIR HATS AND
OTHER PARAPHERNALIA AS WIND WHIPS IN

FROM OUTSIDE. JOHN AND MRS HASSAL HELP TO
HOLD DOWN ESTHER'S VEIL AND TRAIN. RAIN
STARTS TO FALL ON THE TIN ROOF)

MR GILLET:

(TO TETTAWONGA) A summer storm. Won't last …

(TETTAWONGA NODS HIS HEAD AS THE
DIDGERIDOO PULSE BUILDS OMINOUSLY. A
LARGE TREE OUTSIDE IS LIT AND EXPOSED AS
THE LIGHTENING HOLDS DRAMATICALLY.

SFX OF THE RAIN ON THE ROOF GROWS AND THE
SIGNING OF THE REGISTER COMPLETES. A HUGE
ROUND OF APPLAUSE GOES UP FROM THE
GUESTS AND THE NEW MRS WOOLCOT WITH HER
HUSBAND MINGLE EXCITEDLY AMONG THE
GUESTS)

(BLACKOUT AND SILENCE)

(END OF SCENE)

ACT ONE   SCENE 2

'MISRULE' – INTERIOR - EARLY EVENING.

THE SIGN AT THE CENTRE OF THE PROSCENIUM
ARCH NOW READS, 'MISRULE'. THE WORD IS
TIPPED ON AN ANGLE AS IF BROKEN. BENEATH IT
READS THE WORDS, 'ON SYDNEY'S PARRAMATTA
RIVER - THREE YEARS LATER'.

(THE BACKING CLOTH RISES TO REVEAL 'MISRULE'. A FOYER/HALLWAY SITTING AT THE FOOT OF A TIRED BUT GRAND STAIRCASE LEADING TO A DRESS CIRCLE SECOND FLOOR WALKWAY. THE MASTER BEDROOM LEADS OFF THE PROMPT END WHILE THREE DOORS SIT SIDE BY SIDE NEAR THE OFF PROMPT SIDE. NAMES ON DOORS READ, 'PIP/BUNTY, MEG/JUDY, NELL/BABY, RESPECTIVELY.

AT GROUND LEVEL IS THE DINING ROOM [PROMPT], THE NURSERY [OFF PROMPT]. A SWING DOOR OFF THE HALL LEADS TO THE KITCHEN AREA NEAR A FURTHER ACCESS TO THE REAR OF THE HOUSE. OUTSIDE THE DINING ROOM IS A VICTORIAN DESK, AND HALL STAND. SEVERAL SHELVES ARE ON A WALL. AN IMAGINARY FRONT DOOR, WHICH SQUEAKS AND GROANS WHEN OPENED, IS APPROACHED BY STEPS FROM BELOW, TRADITIONALLY THE ORCHESTRA PIT, A DOORSTEP MARKS THE SPOT.

TWO SHORT QUARTER WIDTH FLANKS EXTEND AT EACH SIDE OF THE STAGE INTO THE AUDITORIUM)

AT RISE:

LIGHTS UP. FIRST FOCUS IS ON THE NURSERY WHERE A BARE TABLE, SIX CHAIRS, A HIGH CHAIR FOR THE GENERAL, AN OLD KITCHEN CUPBOARD AND OTHER BASICS ARE SET. A CUCKOO CLOCK HANGS FROM A WALL. SIX CHILDREN ARE FROZEN CAMEO PHOTO-SHOOT STYLE, SITTING POSED AROUND THE TABLE. THE

30

CHILDREN COME TO LIFE AS THEIR FATHER
CALLS FROM UPSTAIRS.

WOOLCOT:

(O. S.) (BELLOWS) MARTHA!

(IRISH HOUSEKEEPER MARTHA RUSHES TO AND
FRO - NOW HEADING ACROSS THE HALL
CARRYING A SMALL CHILD TOWARD THE
NURSERY DOOR)

MARTHA:

(SHOUTS BACK UP THE STAIRS WITH
AFFECTIONATE DISRESPECT) Yes, sir?

(NOT STOPPING, SHE FLINGS OPEN THE NURSERY
DOOR, WHICH STAYS OPEN. PIP IS DRESSED IN
HIS GRAMMAR SCHOOL UNIFORM. JUDY SITS AT
THE HEAD WHERE SHE HAS BEEN MOPING WITH
THE OTHERS)

WOOLCOT:

(O.S.) (UNSEEN IN THE UPSTAIRS MASTER
BEDROOM OFF THE STAIRS) WHEEERE… are the
children?

(MARTHA QUICKLY PASSES THE CHILD TO JUDY
WHO STANDS HIM ON THE TABLE. SHE HURRIES
OUT OF THE NURSERY, CALLING BACK TO
WOOLCOT ON THE WAY)

MARTHA:

About to have tea…sir?

(MARTHA RUSHES ACROSS THE FOYER TO THE
DINING ROOM AT THE OPPOSITE END,
COLLECTING A TRAY WITH GLASSES AND
ACCOUTREMENTS FROM THE DESK AS SHE
PASSES)

(IN THE NURSERY)

JUDY:

(ADDRESSING THE OTHERS) I'll pleasure you all to
know that we are now in the illustrious company of the
famous seventh Woolcot....none other than FRANCIS
RUPERT BURNAND WOOLCOT, ...the 'LITTLE
GENERAL'. (SHE SALUTES)

(THE OTHERS SALUTE AND THE GENERAL
SALUTES BACK)

NELL:

Welcome sir! You sure LOOK like a general!

JUDY:

Probably KNOWS more than the average general?

PIP:

And TALKS more than the average general.

MEG:

But OUR general is NOT average.

BABY:

Hee'th little.

WOOLCOT:

(O.S.) They should have finished tea by now.

(MARTHA RUSHES OUT THE DINING ROOM DOOR, BACK TO THE NURSERY)

MARTHA:

(AS SHE ENTERS, CALLING LOUDLY) Yes, sir. (TO THE CHILDREN) Now come on, you lot, tonight is important. … Your father's first formal dinner party at 'Misrule'.

BUNTY:

Who's coming?

MEG:

Colonel Bryant.

BUNTY:

Oh, him.

JUDY:

Be respectful now. He's father's Commanding Officer, don'cha know.

BUNTY:

He's boring.

(BUNTY LOOKS AT THE BARE TABLE WITH DISDAIN, GETS UP AND EXITS THE NURSERY UNNOTICED BY MARTHA WHO REACHES INTO A CUPBOARD FOR CHILDREN'S PLATES)

JUDY:

He's brave. He saved India, and the Sudan... not to mention the British Empire.

PIP:
> Who said?

JUDY:
> He did. (TO THE GENERAL) Did you know sir, that our
> father and your mother are having roast fowl, three
> vegetables, and four kinds of pudding?

> (THE GENERAL NODS HIS HEAD AS IF TO SAY
> "YES")

PIP:
> It isn't fair.

> (THE GENERAL SHAKES HIS HEAD TO SAY "NO")

MEG:
> But we had dinner at one o'clock. Yours is saved, as usual.

PIP:
> Yes, boiled mutton and carrots.

> (WOOLCOT CALLS DOWN IN BLIND PANIC)

WOOLCOT:
> (O.S.) Stone the crows! MARTHA! Colonel Bryant's
> carriage is at the gates. They'll be here any minute ...

MARTHA:
> (CUPPING HER HANDS FOR AMPLIFICATION)
> Coming, sir.

> (IN THE FOYER)

(IN NO HURRY, BUNTY, DRAGS HIS FEET. WITH A
FACE FILLED WITH CAKE HE CASUALLY PASSES
THE FOOT OF THE STAIRS ON HIS WAY FROM THE
KITCHEN.

ESTHER EMERGES ON TO THE UPSTAIRS DRESS-
CIRCLE STRUGGLING WITH THE BACKOF HER
DRESS)

ESTHER:
Oh, heavens no. Why now? (CALLING HER HUSBAND)
John? (LOUDER) John?

(WOOLCOT IN CIVILIAN DRESS EXITS THE
MARITAL BEDROOM TO HELP ESTHER. HE SEES
BUNTY BELOW)

WOOLCOT:
(ANGRILY TO BUNTY) Why aren't you eating yet?

BUNTY:
(SPLUTTERING THROUGH HIS CAKE) But I am, sir.

(THE BROKEN DOORBELL JANGLES LOUDLY.
BUNTY IS NEAREST TO THE IMAGINARY FRONT
DOOR. NONCHALANTLY HE BEGINS TO OPEN IT)

BUNTY:
(WITH EYES TO THE FLOOR, FACE FILLED WITH
CAKE, HE SLOWLY LOOKS UP TO RECEIVE AN
AWFUL SHOCK. HE EYES THE OMINOUS COLONEL
BRYANT (ALSO IN CIVILIAN DRESS) STANDING
AT THE HEAD OF THE GUESTS, MRS BYANT
SLIGHTLY BEHIND HIM TO ONE SIDE, WITH MISS
BURTON AND DR GORMISTON AT THE REAR.

BUNTY IS TOO STUNNED TO SPEAK. HE TRIES
BUT NO WORDS COME. IN FRIGHT HE RUNS OFF,
BACK TO THE NURSERY. AS HE LEAVES THE
WORDS ARRIVE) CRIPES!! It's HIM!!

(WOOLCOT CONTINUES BATTLE WITH ESTHER'S
ZIP AT THE TOP OF THE STAIRS. FROM THE
DOORSTEP, THE BRYANTS LOOK UP, BECOME
PRIVY TO THE DEBACLE, SHAKE THEIR HEADS
SCORNFULLY AND LOOK AWAY)

BRYANT:
Oh, dear, oh, dear.

MRS BRYANT:
How embarrassing the lower ranks have become …

(MARTHA RE-ENTERS THE FOYER IN TIME TO SEE
BRYANT STRIDING INSIDE UNINVITED. HE IS
FOLLOWED BY MRS BRYANT AND THE OTHERS)

MARTHA:
(AWKWARDLY) Good evening, sir … good evening
madam …

THE GUESTS:
(ONE BY ONE) Good evening Martha.
(THE GUESTS MILL ABOUT THE FOYER AS
MARTHA COLLECTS A TRAY CONTAINING A
SHERRY DECANTER AND CRYSTAL GLASSES
FROM A HALLWAY SHELF, CARRYING IT TO THE
DESK)

MISS BURTON:
(POMPOUSLY AND DRAWN OUT) Chil-dren! …

(MARTHA NEARLY DROPS THE TRAY. MISS
BURTON HOLDS COURT, SPEAKING TO THE
OTHERS AS IF MARTHA DOES NOT EXIST)

BRYANT:

(TO HIS WIFE, REFERRING TO MARTHA) I am told
she's very IN…expensive. (A PAUSE) (TO MISS
BURTON) You were saying, Miss Burton…?

MISS BURTON:

(SUPERIOR AND SANCTIMONIOUS) [Children] …
must be SEEN and not HEARD…

(THE CHILDREN SNEAK OUT OF THE NURSERY,
JUDY HOLDING THE GENERAL'S HAND. THEY
MEET BUNTY ON HIS RETURN, WHO JOINS, AND
ALL WATCH FROM NEAR THE NURSERY DOOR,
UNNOTICED. JUDY MIMICKS MISS BURTON AS
SHE SPEAKS)

MISS BURTON:

Weeell… at my ACADEMY in the Blue Mountains, the
pupils stay for as long as they please…subject of course, to
their parent's bank accounts. My academy is really a
'finishing school'. Some of the 'gels' are less advanced
than others and it takes longer for them to be……finished,
so to speak.

BRYANT:

I'm afraid I'm frightfully old fashioned when it comes to
the education of young 'gels'. I mean…I don't think they
should be educated at all…, fills their heads with all sorts
of silly ideas.

(UNAWARE OF THE SITUATION AT THE TOP OF
THE STAIRS, MARTHA COVERS FOR HER
EMPLOYERS)

MARTHA:
(TO THE GUESTS) Captain Woolcot and Mrs Woolcot
crave your indulgences and have asked me to convey their
most humble apologies on behalf of...er...themselves...
Said Captain and Mrs Woolcot have been delayed and
invite yous...through me...to partake of sherry (SHE
GESTURES TOWARD THE DECANTER AND
GLASSES SET ON THE DESK IN AN ALCOVE NEAR
THE DINING ROOM ENTRANCE)... 'til they
imminent...appear!

(MARTHA NOTICES THE GUEST'S
PREOCCUPATION WITH THE STAIRCASE)

MARTHA:
....which they 'ave. Oh, lordie me.

BRYANT:
Thank you, Martha. (COLONEL BRYANT IS QUICKLY
IN CHARGE OF THE SHERRY DECANTER AS
MARTHA ATTEMPTS TO REACH FOR IT ON THE
DESK)

BRYANT:
Sherry, Miss Burton?

MISS BURTON:
(GRATEFUL) Just a drop, colonel... (HE POURS) No... a
little more than that, if you would be so kind? Thank you
so much.

(BRYANT FILLS THE GLASSES)

DR GORMISTON:
(RAISING HIS GLASS) To the suppression of unruly children.

MISS BURTON:
Here, here!

BRYANT:
Now I'll drink to that!

MARTHA:
(TO HERSELF) You'd drink to any-thing, you pickled old soak.

MRS BRYANT:
(COCKING HER HEAD) So sorry, dear, I missed that. What did you say?

MARTHA:
I said … (THINKING).... the drink isn't just any old thing … and the crystal's not broke.

BRYANT:
(THE SMELL UNDER HIS NOSE STRONGER NOW) Thank you….Martha?

(MARTHA BOWS AND BACKS OUT OF THE FOYER TO THE KITCHEN AS IF THEY ARE ROYALTY, ALMOST IMMEDIATELY RETURNING TO THE NURSERY WITH BREAD, TEA AND MELTING BUTTER. THE CHILDREN SEE HER AND RUSH TO THE TABLE JUST IN TIME FOR MARTHA TO SET IT DOWN.

WOOLCOT, UNAWARE OF THE CONVERSATION BELOW, FINALLY SORTS ESTHER'S DRESS. AT HER BEHEST THEY ADOPT A PICTURE POSTCARD POSE AT THE TOP OF THE STAIRS AS IF ROYALTY, ABOUT TO MAKE A GRAND ENTRANCE. MARTHA, NOW RETURNING FROM THE NURSERY, LOOKS UP AND APPLAUDS LOUDLY. SHE IS FOLLOWED OUT BY THE CHILDREN WHO RETURN UN-NOTICED TO THEIR WATCHING POSITION NEAR THE NURSERY DOOR. ALL NOW LOOK TO THE STAIRCASE, JOIN IN THE APPLAUSE, THOUGH CYNICALLY FOR SOME. MARTHA IS FIXATED ON ESTHER.

THE APPLAUSE CONTINUES AS WOOLCOT AND ESTHER EXUDE GRAND ELEGANCE AND GRACE DESCENDING THE ONCE GRAND STAIRCASE. THE GUESTS CATCH A GLIMPSE OF THE CHILDREN WHO, ON SEEING MARTHA COMING THEIR WAY, NOISILY BANG AND CRASH INTO ONE ANOTHER RETURNING AGAIN TO THE NURSERY.

RE-SEATED, BUNTY, WITH HIS INSATIABLE APPETITE, STUFFS HIMSELF AS THE OTHER DISGRUNTLED FACES LOOK AT THE FOOD MOST DISAPPROVINGLY.

THE WOOLCOTS ARRIVE AT THE FOOT OF THE STAIRS)

MARTHA:
(HER EYES STILL FIXED ON ESTHER) WOW!
Doesn't you look the business!

WOOLCOT:

(DISAPPROVING) Martha?

MARTHA:

(WITH HER USUAL LICENSE) Yes, sir? (WOOLCOT IGNORES HER)

(WE DO NOT HEAR AS THE WOOLCOTS FORMALLY GREET THEIR GUESTS, USHERING THEM TOWARD THE DINING ROOM WITH MARTHA'S HELP. MARTHA THEN TURNS AND HEADS BACK INTO THE KITCHEN)

(IN THE NURSERY)

PIP:

Urrgh!

(BUNTY GRABS ANOTHER PIECE OF BREAD)

BUNTY:

Come on… what you waiting for? Two, four, six, eight. Bog in, don't wait!

JUDY:

(LOOKING AT THEIR LOT) Bread and butter! Urrgh! While the others have roast fowl. Not fair!

(IN THE DINING ROOM)

WOOLCOT:

(GESTURING TO THE TABLE) Please, do be seated....

(THE GUESTS ARE SHOWN TO THEIR SEATS BY THE HOSTS. THE CONTRAST BETWEEN DINING

ROOM AND NURSERY IS PRONOUNCED.
WOOLCOT, ESTHER, BRYANT, MRS BRYANT, DR
GORMISTON AND MISS BURTON SIT AT A LARGE
VICTORIAN OAK TABLE. THE BEST SILVER AND
CRYSTAL INCLUDING FILLED WINE GOBLETS,
HAVE BEEN LAID OUT. THE GUESTS FINISH
SERVING VEGETABLES TO THEIR PLATES FROM
SILVER WARMERS.

MARTHA RE-ENTERS THE DINING ROOM
CARRYING A LARGE COVERED SILVER SERVER
CONTAINING A ROAST TURKEY. SHE PLACES IT
RESPECTFULLY BEFORE WOOLCOT WHO
ACKNOWLEDGES IT AND BOWS HIS HEAD FOR
'GRACE'. THE OTHERS FOLLOW HIS EXAMPLE,
EACH BOWING THEIR HEADS, INCLUDING
MARTHA WHO SHOWS RESPECT TO THE LORD
STANDING, WHILST AT THE SAME TIME TAKING
THE GUEST'S PLATES TO WOOLCOT READIED TO
RECEIVE THE TURKEY)

WOOLCOT:
For what we are about to receive may the Lord …...

(WOOLCOT IS OVER-RIDDEN BY A LOUD VOICE
FROM THE OTHER SIDE OF THE HOUSE. THE
GUESTS LOOK UP, AND THEN DOWN AGAIN)

PIP:
(LOUDLY FROM THE NURSERY) My father and Esther
are having roast fowl, three vegetables, and four kinds of
pudding! (HE LEAVES THE TABLE, THE FIRST TO
DO SO)

WOOLCOT:

… make us truly thankful. Amen.

ALL:

Amen.

(WOOLCOT AND ESTHER TRY TO IGNORE PIP'S OUTBURST AS HE LIFTS THE HOT LID. THROUGH THE STEAM IS REVEALED ROAST FOWL. HE STARTS TO CARVE AS THERE COMES A TIMID KNOCK ON THE DOOR. ALL EYES TURN AS IT SLOWLY OPENS AND PIP'S HEAD PROTRUDES. HE ENTERS CAUTIOUSLY, AN EMPTY PLATE HELD OUT BEFORE HIM TO THE SURPRISE OF THE FACES AT THE TABLE)

PIP:

(VERY NERVOUS) Excuse me, father? May I have some roast fowl?

(WOOLCOT CAN BARELY HIDE HIS FURY)

WOOLCOT:

(CARVING A SMALL PIECE) Yes, Pip…just a little. (TO THE GUESTS) My eldest son, Philip.

(THE GUESTS LOOK SANCTIMONIOUSLY TOLERANT AS PIP IS SERVED)

WOOLCOT:

Good night, Pip!

(THE DOOR CLOSES AND THERE IS AN EMBARRASSED LULL IN CONVERSATION,

BROKEN BY THE SOUND OF METAL ON METAL AS
WOOLCOT RESUMES CARVING)

ESTHER:
(BREAKING THE SILENCE) We hear such excellent
reports of your Academy in the Blue Mountains, Miss
Burton. To what do you attribute your enormous success?

MISS BURTON:
(POMPOUSLY) Well … it's difficult to know where to
start....

(THERE IS ANOTHER GENTLE KNOCK AT THE
DOOR. THE ROOM GOES DEATHLY QUIET. ALL
FACES FIX TO THE DOOR WHICH OPENS AND
NELL'S ANGELIC FACE APPEARS)

WOOLCOT:
Yes, Nell?

(NELL IS TERRIFIED AND DOESN'T MOVE)

ESTHER:
(HELPING HER DESPERATE HUSBAND) Come in
Nell, but be quick. What is it?

(BRYANT TAKES A SHINE TO NELL AND SMILES
GRATUITOUSLY. HE BECKONS HER WITH HIS
FOREFINGER. SHE ENTERS WITH ONE HAND
BEHIND HER BACK)

BRYANT:
Well, my little maid, won't you shake hands with me?

(HE INTRODUCES HIS OWN HAND TO THAT OF NELL'S BEHIND HER BACK)

WOOLCOT:

What a little barbarian you are, Nell? Show us your hand?

(THE PLATE IS REVEALED)

NELL:

(TO BRYANT) I thought father might give me some fowl too. (TO WOOLCOT) Just a leg, or a wing, or a….

WOOLCOT:

(EXPLODING) What is the meaning of this?

(ESTHER LOOKS TO TRY TO CALM HIM. SHE GESTURES TO NELL TO APPROACH HER FATHER WHO SAVAGELY SEVERS A LEG AND BANGS IT ONTO HER PLATE. MARTHA REACTS BUT DOES NOT INTERFERE)

WOOLCOT:

Now back to the nursery. I don't know what has possessed you both tonight!

(NELL DAINTILY WALKS AWAY. IN A FLASH OF INSPIRATION, AS SHE REACHES THE DOOR SHE TURNS BACK)

NELL:

If you would just give me a wing for poor Meg…and there's Baby…and Bunty…?

WOOLCOT:

Be OFF! GOOD NIGHT!

(THE DOOR CLOSES QUICKLY BEHIND HER. THE
SILENCE PUNCTUATES THE TENSION AS
WOOLCOT CARVES THE BIRD ROUGHLY, AND
MARTHA COMPLETES SERVING THE GUESTS)

MRS BRYANT:
(SIPPING HER WINE AND STUDYING THE GLASS
AS SHE TRIES TO CHANGE THE SUBJECT) I
understand that the medicinal qualities in Australian red
wine are well noted. I have it on good authority that…

(A SHARP LOUD KNOCK SOUNDS FROM THE
DOOR. ALL EYES FIX AGAIN AS IT IS FLUNG OPEN
FROM THE OUTSIDE. THE LITTLE GENERAL,
BOWL IN HAND STANDS IN THE DOORWAY AS A
HAND REACHES OUT AND PUSHES HIM INTO THE
ROOM. ALL ARE AGHAST AS JUDY RUNS INTO
THE ROOM, GRABS THE GENERAL WHO DROPS
THE BOWL, AND HURRIES OUT.

WOOLCOT LEAPS FROM HIS CHAIR AND
EXPLODES, ACCOMPANIED BY THE SLAMMING
OF THE DOOR AND SOUNDS OF RUNNING FEET)

WOOLCOT:
(EXPLODING) CHILDREN! (SHAKING) CHILDREN!!

BRYANT:
Contrary and cantankerous,

MISS BURTON:
Obstreperous and rancorous,

BRYANT:
Illogical and ignorant,

(ESTHER CAN'T BELIEVE WHAT SHE IS HEARING)

MISS BURTON:
>Asinine, capricious, perverse and avaricious,

MRS BRYANT:
>Their proclivities unpleasant,

MISS BURTON:
>Their manners a disgrace!

(ESTHER TRIES TO REASON)

ESTHER:
>But then one day they'll drift away,
>when they decide to leave us…
>I'm told such things occasionally occur…

DR GORMISTON:
>Yes. And... speaking from experience I have to ask, would their departure break your heart?

ESTHER:
>(STARTS TO SPEAK) Well …

WOOLCOT:
>(BELLOWS – INTERRUPTING ESTHER) Not likely!
>NO SIR! CHILDREN! (MORE SUBDUED) CHILDREN!

(MEANWHILE, IN THE NURSERY)

JUDY:
>Angelical and lovable, affectionate and sweet…

CHILDREN:
We're the nicest people you'd ever want to meet...

JUDY:
Just look at me?

MEG:
and me?

PIP:
and me?

NELL:
and me?

PIP:
(POINTING TO BUNTY) ...and him?

BABY:
and me?

CHILDREN:
We're as good as good can be!

(LIGHTS FLASH BETWEEN ROOMS)

WOOLCOT:
Shameless!

CHILDREN:
Blameless!

WOOLCOT:
Lawless!

CHILDREN:
Flawless!

WOOLCOT:
Fearful!

CHILDREN:
Cheerful!

BRYANT:
Devastating!

CHILDREN:
Captivating!

MRS BRYANT:
Alarming!

CHILDREN:
Charming!

MISS BURTON:
Frightful!

CHILDREN:
Delightful!

WOOLCOT:
Deplorable!

JUDY:
(WITH THAT KNOWING LOOK) …adorable…

(WOOLCOT IS APOPLECTIC. HE FLIES OUT OF THE
DINING ROOM, INTO THE NURSERY, RIPPING UP

HIS RIDING CROP FROM THE HALL STAND AS HE
PASSES. HE STORMS IN TO FACE THE CHILDREN
SITTING INNOCENTLY AT THE TABLE, THE
GENERAL, ON THE TABLE IN FRONT OF JUDY.
WOOLCOT LIFTS PIP UP BY THE HAIR,
THRASHING HIM ABOUT THE LEGS. PIP'S PLATE
CRASHES TO THE GROUND AS JUDY TRIES TO
WEDGE HERSELF BETWEEN PIP AND WOOLCOT'S
VIOLENT STROKES. MEG LIFTS THE NOW CRYING
GENERAL OUT OF HARM'S WAY AND BEFRIENDS
BABY AND NELL COWERING IN A CORNER)

JUDY:

It was ME, father! Leave them alone. I put them up to it!

(IN THE DINING ROOM THE RIGHTEOUS FACES OF
THE GUESTS CONTRAST WITH THE DISTRAUGHT
BUT BARELY DIGNIFIED ESTHER)

WOOLCOT:

There will be NO pantomime tomorrow! I am sending your
tickets to the Digby-Smiths!

JUDY:

Not the Digby-Smiths, father?

WOOLCOT:

ENOUGH, JUDITH! You are all confined to quarters. No
visits. No visitors. No riding. Noooo PANTOMIME!

(SLAMMING THE DOOR ON HIS WAY OUT, THE
CUCKOO CLOCK ANNOUNCES THE TURN OF THE
HOUR)

(BACK IN THE DINING ROOM)

ESTHER:

Will you excuse me, please?
(DR GORMISTON AND BRYANT RISE AS ESTHER
STANDS AND TRIES TO LEAVE GRACEFULLY.
BRYANT THEN TUCKS INTO DINNER AS IF
NOTHING HAS HAPPENED)

BRYANT:

I say, this fowl is AWFULLY good, what?

(HIS BEHAVIOUR CONTRASTS WITH THE
DISMAYED FACES OF THE LADIES AND DR
GORMISTON.

(IN THE NURSERY)

JUDY:

(TO MEG) At least we'll miss French class.

(WOOLCOT HEARS THIS, AND TURNS. THE DOOR
FLIES OPEN AND HE SHOUTS ACROSS TO JUDY)

WOOLCOT:

You will attend French class on Saturday as usual! And
Judith… the General will be YOUR responsibility!

(EXCHANGING LOOKS, ESTHER BRUSHES PAST
HIM AS SHE ENTERS TO COMFORT THE
CHILDREN. THEY ALL GATHER AROUND HER)

JUDY:

(TO ESTHER) It was MY fault. Why does he punish us
ALL? It was only a bit of fun.

MEG:

Couldn't you get 'round him, Esther?

PIP:

Be a good fellow, Essie. (PATTING HER ON THE BACK)

ESTHER:

I think this time, it's going to be up to you. Look, I'll try to shorten confinement to barracks … but you must help me.

NELL:

But how, Esther?

ESTHER:

Come closer. (THEY CROWD IN AND SHE WHISPERS SOMETHING TO THEM. THEY SHAKE THEIR HEADS AS ONE, AS IF IT IS NOT POSSIBLE, THEN SHAKE, YES. ESTHER CALLS THEM TO ORDER) Come on now… bedtime, and … prayers?
(CHILDREN EXIT, ESTHER HOLDING THE HANDS OF BABY AND NELL, JUDY CARRYING GENERAL)

(LIGHTS FADE)

(END OF SCENE)

ACT ONE　　　　　SCENE 3

WOOLCOT'S STUDY – EARLY MORNING

THE SIGN AMID THE PROSCENIUM ARCH NOW READS 'SATURDAY MORNING'.

(A PARTNER'S DESK LOOKS OUT THROUGH OPEN
FRENCH WINDOWS TO THE VERANDAH, THE
WILLOW, AND THE RIVER BEYOND. A WALL OF
BOOKSHELVES, AN UPRIGHT PIANO AND
OCCASIONAL CHAIRS MAKE UP THE FURNITURE.
WOOLCOT, RESPLENDENT IN POLO OUTFIT,
PRACTICES A SHOT. UNSEEN BY WOOLCOT,
MARTHA ENTERS, PICKING UP THE MORNING
TEA TRAY AS HE HITS)

MARTHA:
Good shot, sir.

(A STARTLED WOOLCOT SPINS AROUND TO FACE
MARTHA)

WOOLCOT:
(BUSINESSLIKE) Martha…the children will be home
after French. Please see they do NOT leave the house.

(ESTHER ENTERS BEHIND HIM DRESSED
BEAUTIFULLY FOR THE POLO. MARTHA IS FIRST
TO SEE HER)

MARTHA:
(WITH USUAL LICENSE) My! You look lovely. So
fresh. A real pitcha.

ESTHER:
(SMILING) Why thank you, Martha.

MARTHA:
(MAKING THE MOST OF THE MOMENT) Nobody'll
bother with the stupid polo …they'll all be looking at you.
(TURNING TO WOOLCOT) Isn't that so, sir?

WOOLCOT:

Thank you, Martha. THAT will be ALL.

MARTHA:

(CHEERFULLY, KNOWING SHE IS INDESPENSABLE) Thank you, sir.

ESTHER:

(MARTHA EXITS. WOOLCOT SIGHS)

WOOLCOT:

I suppose it would be impossible to replace Martha?

ESTHER:

(SMOTHERS A SMILE) I'm afraid so, who else would last a week with the children?

WOOLCOT:

Who else indeed? Though for once, I agree with her. The young subalterns will certainly have an eye for you.

(THERE IS A KNOCK ON THE DOOR. IT OPENS AND PIP ENTERS, NOW IN NEAT CASUAL DRESS. WOOLCOT TURNS TO HIM, NOT SURE WHAT TO EXPECT)

WOOLCOT:

Hrmph…well? What do you want, Pip?

PIP:

I came to study, sir. I feel a bit backward with my mathematics, and I don't want to waste any opportunity when I'm costing you so much in school fees.

(WOOLCOT LOOKS AT PIP, FROM THE POINT OF
VIEW THAT HE IS BEING SET UP)

WOOLCOT:

Is that so? Well…there are some sets of problems in that
(POINTS) drawer there. I did them when I was at school. If
you think they'll be of some use…

PIP:

(QUICKLY MOVING TO THE DESK AND TAKING
THEM OUT) Thanks awfully…I'm sure they'll be a great
help.

(WOOLCOT LOOKS AT PIP WHO SITS DOWN AT
THE DESK AND STARTS WORKING. HE IS
PERPLEXED AND UNSURE OF WHAT IS
HAPPENING)

PIP:

How very neatly and correctly you worked, father. I
wonder if I'll ever get to be as good as this?

WOOLCOT:

(TAKEN IN AND PLEASED HE CAN BE PROUD OF
SOMETHING) Don't be discouraged, Pip. I WAS rather
beyond the other boys in my class in these subjects, I
remember. We can't all excel in the same things, and I'm
glad to see you are beginning to realize the importance of
work.

PIP:

Yes, father.

(MEG KNOCKS GENTLY AND ENTERS, CARRYING
SOME SHEET MUSIC)

MEG:

Father, you've often mentioned that your music is falling
to pieces. I thought I might restore them while you play
polo … sorry... I mean... while you win at polo today.
Would that be all right … please?

(WOOLCOT LOOKS HARD AT MEG NOW SURE HE
IS BEING SOFTENED UP. MEG SMILES BACK
BEAUTIFULLY, UNSETTLING HIM. SHE REACHES
UP TO A SHELF AND STARTS FILING THE MUSIC
SHEETS NEATLY)

WOOLCOT:

Thank you, Margaret. They do need attention. I suppose
there is no time like the present.

(NELL AND BABY APPEAR AT THE DOOR EACH
CARRYING A TRAY FOR MORNING TEA. THEY
WALK IN AND STAND BEFORE THEIR FATHER)

NELL:

We thought you would like a little morning tea, father.

(PIP AND MEG ARE SEIZED BY A SUDDEN
COUGHING FIT AS WOOLCOT LOOKS AT THEM
FLABBERGASTED.

SFX OF A SCYTHE CUTTING AND SWISHING
THROUGH LONG GRASS EMANATES FROM OFF
STAGE. WOOLCOT STEPS TO THE FRENCH
WINDOWS, LOOKS OUT AND BECOMES
ALARMED)

WOOLCOT:

(CALLING INTO THE GARDEN) Good heavens, Helen, you'll cut your legs off!

(ESTHER, CARRYING THE GENERAL, ENTERS THE ROOM)

JUDY:

(O.S.) Oh, no father – I'm an old hand at this!

(WOOLCOT SMILES TO HIMSELF BUT THE SMILE TRANSFORMS INSTANTLY TO RAGE AS HE WATCHES)

JUDY:

(O.S.) Whoops?

(WOOLCOT REACTS AS SFX OF HIS PRIZED ROSEBUSH FALLING LOUDLY TO THE GROUND IS HEARD. MARTHA RE-ENTERS, LOOKING FOR THE TRAYS)

WOOLCOT:

My prize rosebush! Stop immediately, Helen!

JUDY:

(O.S.) Accidents WILL happen, even to the best grass-cutters! (TO HERSELF) An' I was just doing it to pleasure him…

WOOLCOT:

(HEARING HER AND SHOUTING DOWN) Well it won't 'pleasure him' to have to provide you with cork legs and re-stock the garden!

(HE SHAKES HIS HEAD IN DESPAIR, WALKS BACK
INSIDE THROUGH THE FRENCH WINDOWS AND
LOOKS DOWN AT THE MORNING TEA ON HIS
DESK)

WOOLCOT:
(TO ESTHER) WHAT... is going on in this house?

(ESTHER PUTS GENERAL DOWN THEN TRIES TO
PACIFY HER HUSBAND AS MARTHA PICKS UP THE
TWO TRAYS AND EXITS)

ESTHER:
John…they are trying, trying…to tell you something.

MARTHA:
(ON THE WAY OUT) (TO HERSELF) Oh lordie...this
was such a happy home…

(WOOLCOT SHAKES HIS HEAD IN DISBELIEF AS
HE EXITS THE ROOM, PASSING JUDY WHO
ENTERS. HE PAUSES, LOOKS AS IF TO SAY
SOMETHING, THEN CHANGES HIS MIND AND
RACES OUT)

ESTHER:
(TO CHILDREN) Come on, all of you. You are trying so
hard and that is to be commended. (MORE URGENT) Oh,
no! … Have you forgotten about French? Your ferry will
be heading back to the Quay any minute now.

JUDY:
(LOOKING GLOOMY) Don't worry, Essie. We're ready.
(LOOKING TO THE OTHERS) Aren't we?

(THEIR HEADS DROOP AND ALL SKULK
UNHAPPILY FROM THE ROOM AT THE THOUGHT
OF FRENCH)

MARTHA:
(TO ESTHER AS THEY LEAVE) I do hope Colonel
Bryant's team excels at the polo.

ESTHER:
(BETWEEN THE TWO OF THEM) And Captain John
Woolcot... in particular.

(LIGHTS FADE)

(END OF SCENE)

ACT ONE   SCENE 4

ON THE TRAM

THE SIGN AMID THE PROSCENIUM ARCH NOW
READS, 'THE FRENCH LESSON'.

(NOISY, LAUGHING YOUNG ADULTS RIDE AN
EARLY SYDNEY 'TOAST RACK' ELECTRIC TRAM
TO THE FRENCH LESSON. THE TRAM IS SET AT AN
ANGLE TO THE AUDIENCE TO PROVIDE THE BEST
SIGHTLINE TO SOME OF THE KEY PASSENGERS.
SEATING IS ARRANGED BETWEEN SEVERAL
DUET SETS OF FACING BENCHES AS EXISTED AT
THE TIME, MOUNTED HIGH ON A TRUCK. A
CONDUCTOR RUNS ALONG THE LENGTH OF THE
TRAM ON A 'FOOT BOARD' [RUNNING BOARD
THAT KEEPS ALL HEADS ABOUT THE SAME

HEIGHT] STAGE FRONT. THE PHYSICAL TRAM
UNIT IS A TRUCK THAT MOVES ON WHEELS.

THE TRAM SITS FIXED, FOR THE MOST PART,
BEFORE A MOVING PROJECTION WHOSE IMAGES
COVER THE SCENIC JOURNEY FROM CIRCULAR
QUAY, INTO BRIDGE STREET, THENCE INTO
ELIZABETH, TURNING INTO WILLIAM, JOINING
OXFORD STREET TOWARDS VICTORIA
BARRACKS, THE TRAMSHEDS AT THE JUNCTION,
THENCE DOWN BONDI ROAD TO BONDI BEACH.
THE CONDUCTOR IS A NEW AUSTRALIAN, A
COMIC CHARACTER WHO STRUGGLES WITH
OCKER AUSTRALIAN LANGUAGE. HIS BACK IS
OFTEN TO THE AUDIENCE AS HE REACHES INTO
BAYS OF SEATED PASSENGERS COLLECTING
FARES AND HANDING OUT TICKETS. THE TRAM'S
DESTINATION READS: 'CIRCULAR QUAY – BONDI
BEACH')

AT RISE:

THE SCENE OPENS TO THE RING OF THE TRAM
BELL. THE YOUNG FOLK BOARD THE ALMOST
FULL TRAM AT THE OLD CIRCULAR QUAY
TERMINUS.

IN THE FRONT SITS ANDREW COURTNEY. THE
WOOLCOTS, INCLUDING THE GENERAL, SIT
CENTRE. PIP IS DRESSED CASUALLY, AS ARE THE
OTHERS.

SUDDENLY, ALDITH'S UNIQUELY PENETRATING
VOICE BLASTS. LATE, SHE BOARDS LAST,
JAMMING INTO THE FRONT SEATS. SHE SHOUTS

RUDELY OVER THE HEADS OF THE PASSENGERS
WHO ALL REACT.

ALDITH:
(AN OVER THE TOP BITCH) Meg, daaaarling! It's been
centuries?

JUDY:
(REACTING BEFORE MEG CAN SPEAK) Aldith,
daaaaaaarling! It's been three days…actually!

(ALL HEADS TURN AS THE CONVERSATION GOES
BACK AND FORTH)

MEG:
(INTIMIDATED) Hello, Aldith.

ALDITH:
(STILL ADRESSING MEG IN HER SUPERIOR
MANNER AND POINTING AT JUDY) She must be such
a TRIAL for you.

(THE CONDUCTOR HOLDS ON TO THE BRASS
RAILS AS HE MOVES DOWN THE SIDE OF THE
TRAM SELLING HIS TICKETS, STOPPING AT THE
WOOLCOT'S BAY. PIP PAYS FOR ALL THE
WOOCOTS)

CONDUCTOR:
(COMIC CHARACTER) Fez. Fez pliz (TAKING THE
MONEY FROM PIP) That'll be two 'dults... an' two 'alves.
Thanking you, kindly, sir. (BELLOWS) Fez pliz. This
trrram stoppin' aaall stups t' Bondi Beach. Neeext stup,
Maaark Fois!
(HE IS VERY ENTHUSIASTIC WITH THE BELL)

ALDITH:

Dear Margeurite … Have you heard? We're ALL going to Bondi after French. There's skating and a roller coaster, and a merry-go-round. Everyone's coming. Apres le lecon francais, n'est-ce-pas?

(MEG GOES TO ANSWER BUT CAN'T THINK OF ANYTHING TO SAY. THE BELL RINGS AS CONDUCTOR SHOUTS)

CONDUCTOR:

Fez pliz. Stupping aaall stups t' Bondi Beach. This stup, Maaark Fois!

(THE TRAM STOPS. BEATRICE AND JANET CLIMB ABOARD AS BELL RINGS AND TRAM MOVES OFF)

BEATRICE:

(ACROSS THE SEATS) Aldith! Darling!

JANET:

Daaarling.

ALDITH:

Daaaaarlings?

JUDY:

(HER MIND ELSEWHERE) (TO NO-ONE IN PARTICULAR) What's the use of fathers in the world, I'd like to know! (TO PIP) Think of the times we could have if he didn't live with us.

MEG:

Oh, Judy, that's awful!

BUNTY:

We could go to a pantomime seven times a week!

NELL:

Wow!

PIP:

I hope the bloomin' Digby-Smiths tumble over the dress-circle rail before the curtain even rises.

NELL:

It's our pantomime, not theirs.

BABY:

I'th th'pill my 'jaffath' under their t'oeth … to help zem on z'eir vay.

BUNTY:

Not if I got the jaffas first.

(THEY ALL LAUGH)

ALDITH:

(BACK TO MEG) It's going to be magical at Bondi. Are you coming?

JUDY:

(BEFORE MEG CAN ANSWER) We certainly ARE!

MEG:

No, Aldith. We've all been gated.

ALDITH:

(CONDESCENDING) Oooh … poor Margeurite…

BEATRICE:
>   (TO JANET) She's so funny…

JUDY:
>   Hilarious! Like the spider on the dunnee seat!

CONDUCTOR:
>   Fez. All fez pliz. Stuppin' aaall stups t' Bondi Beach.
>   Neeext stup, Tiaaaylor Square.

JUDY:
>   (SHOUTING TO ALDITH) We're not even going to
>   French!

MEG/PIP:
>   Whaaa….?

NELL/BUNTY:
>   We're not?

JUDY:
>   That also.

ALDITH:
>   But you must. You're not civilised with no French in your
>   rep-er-toy-er?

MALE TRAVELLER 1:
>   (IN A VERY SUPERIOR MANNER) Such language?
>
>   (THE PASSENGER BESIDE HIM SHAKES HIS HEAD
>   IN AGREEMENT)

JUDY:
>   Too true! And Aldith?

ALDITH:
   (SCORNFULLY) What?

JUDY:
   (VERY QUICKLY) When you're pedigree's thin and your
   accent is quaint, and aristocratic is something you ain't,
   and you're common and boorish, and vulgar and low…
   Just take yourself.... to Monsieur Marceau! Right NOW!

   (PIP & NELL APPLAUD)

JUDY:
   (PRONOUNCED) … but for us.... NOT today, thank you
   very much. We're off to Bondi! Yeaah!

MALE TRAVELLER 1:
   (HEARING JUDY AND IN A VERY SUPERIOR
   ENGLISH MANNER) Just listen to that! Colonials are so
   very plebian.

MALE TRAVELLER 2:
   But if they drop a word of French they're less
   antipodean… don't you think?

MALE TRAVELLER 3:
   (AUSTRALIAN OCKER) Well …it comes in real useful
   'round Erskinville way. I know for a fact that you'll knock
   'em all dead when you say 'Madamoiselle'. All the sheila's
   will know you're as classy as …. (SCREWS UP HIS
   FACE)

CONDUCTOR:
   This stup, Tiaaaylor Square.

ANDREW:

This is our stop. Monsieur Marceau … here we come!

JUDY:

(GIVES A PERT WAVE) Bye, bye, all.

THE OTHERS GET OFF THE TRAM ALL
MUTTERING ABOUT THE CHANCE THE
WOOLCOTS ARE TAKING)

ALDITH:

(TO MEG) Are you really …

JUDY:

If you ever get to Bondi, Aldith, tell us what you learnt. Ha
ha!

(ALDITH TURNS AND GOES WITH THE OTHERS)

PIP:

Judes. I don't think we better. What about the General?

JUDY:

You'll see....

(THE CONDUCTOR WATCHES THE INDECISION,
HOLDING THE TRAM)

NELL:

Are we getting off or not?

BUNTY:

Yeah. Are we on or off?

CONDUCTOR:

(GETTING ANXIOUS) C'mon. Make up your moinds boiys and goils. We can't a-haaang 'bout 'ere upsettin' the toiimetable, now can we?

JUDY:

We definitely can't. We're staying put!

(CONDUCTOR RINGS THE BELL AND THE TRAM SETS OFF WITH THE WOOLCOTS ON BOARD)

CONDUCTOR:

I like someone 'knows her own moiind. Fez pliz. Stupping aaall stups t' Pad-ding-ton and then t' the Junction and Bondi Beach. Neeext stup, Vic-too-ri-aa Baaa-rra-cks.

BABY:

I fort vee vas going ter Fench.....

MEG:

(INTERRUPTING) We shouldn't be doing this. We really should not!

PIP:

Let's get off next stop and go back.

MEG:

Good idea.

JUDY:

Are you scared? Frightened of a bit of fun?

MEG:

Yes.

JUDY:

Meg... take the others to Bondi. Pip and I will see father minds the General. We'll catch you up.

MEG:

Whaaa.... But that's impossible. Father is playing polo for the regiment!

CONDUCTOR:

This stup, Vic-too-ri-aa Baaa-rra-cks. All alight for Vic-too-ri-aa Baaa-rra-cks.

(THE TRAM/SCENERY STOPS. THE CHILDREN HESITATE AGAIN, INCLUDING JUDY. MEG IS SEVERELY DISTRESSED)

CONDUCTOR:

Aaaw... c'mon kids. Make up your moinds. We can't a-haaang 'bout 'ere upsettin' ….

JUDY:

(RESOLVED, AND FINISHING WITH HIM)....settin' the toiimetable, now can we?

(JUDY CARRIES THE GENERAL AND LEADS PIP CLIMBING DOWN OUT OF THE TRAM)

BABY:

Vere iss vey going?

MEG:

Don't worry, Baby. I'll look after you.
(PIP & JUDY WAVE BACK NERVOUSLY TO THE OTHERS AS THE CONDUCTOR RINGS THE BELL AND THE PHYSICAL TRAM NOW TRUCKS OFF

WHILE THE IMAGE OF THE WALLS AROUND
VICTORIA BARRACKS REMAINS PROJECTED.
WITH THE TRAM GONE WE SEE A TRAM SHELTER
WITH A LONG BENCH ON THE FOOTPATH. IT IS
EMPTY. JUDY TAKES THE GENERAL'S HAND AS
PIP FOLLOWS BEHIND)

JUDY:
(TAKING THE GENERAL'S HAND) Come on General.

(LIGHTS FADE)

(END OF SCENE)

ACT ONE   SCENE 5

THE PARADE GROUND – VICTORIA BARRACKS

AT RISE:

LIGHTS FADE UP. OFF STAGE, A MILITARY BAND
ACCOMPANIES PARADE GROUND SHOUTING.

ON STAGE, SEVERAL MEMBERS OF THE GUARD
ARE MARCHED BY A CORPORAL. A SENTRY
SALUTES)

CORPORAL:
(O.S.) Squad, by the left, quick march... hup, hup...
(coming on stage) hup, hup … Squaaad... 'Alt! Guaaaard
… right turn! H'order h'arms! (THEY ORDER ARMS)
DISMISS!

(THE GUARD GOES OFF STAGE, INTO A GUARD
ROOM, LEAVING THE SENTRY LIKE A
CLOCKWORK SOLDIER. HE RESUMES HIS BEAT.

JUDY & PIP APPEAR, SNEAK UP TO THE GATE AND
HIDE BEHIND THE SENTRY BOX. THEY HAVE
LITTLE GENERAL WITH THEM)

PIP:

Joods, this is the worst thing we've ever done in our lives.
Father will fry us.

JUDY:

I'm in charge. Father said so….and it's only fun. He'll
understand.

PIP:

(NOT AT ALL SURE) Oh, sure. He'll be bloomin'
COURT – MARSHALLED if you ask me!

JUDY:

Do you want to go to Bondi, or not?

PIP:

Of course I do, but to just abandon him …

JUDY:

We're not abandoning him.

PIP:

Then what are we doing?

JUDY:

We're having him minded (PATIENTLY) Look, who is the
General's father... tell me that... ?

PIP:

(TRYING TO KEEP UP WITH HER RAPID FIRE REASONING) Well... Father is …

JUDY:

And isn't it right and proper fathers should look after their sons? And doesn't he deserve we should get even, for doing us out of the pantomime? And isn't the aquarium too much fun to miss?

(SHE WHIPS A PIECE OF PAPER FROM HER DRESS POCKET)

JUDY:

Read that.

PIP:

(READS) "Please take me to Captain Woolcot."

(JUDY TAKES IT BACK, AND PINS IT TO LITTLE GENERAL'S SHIRT)

PIP:

Ohh, Judy … I really don't think we oughta …

JUDY:

Go and keep a look-out for the tram. I'll join you in a minute… go on!

(JUDY IMPATIENTLY SHOOS PIP AWAY, THEN STOOPS AND CUDDLES LITTLE GENERAL)

JUDY:

General, see that nice man over there... the one in the pretty red costume?

(LITTLE GENERAL NODS)

JUDY:

Go and see him. He'll take you to Father, and you can see all the horses. Won't that be fun? (THE GENERAL NODS YES) Of course it will... and your Mama will be there. (JUDY IS TRYING TO OVERCOME HER INSTINCTIVE RESERVATIONS, WHICH ARE GROWING) Give us a hug then, there's a good boy.... (THEY HUG)

PIP:

(DISTANT TRAM BELL SOUNDS AS PIP RE-APPEARS) Joods... the tram!

JUDY:

(TO LITTLE GENERAL) Off you go ...

(JUDY TAKES ONE LAST LOOK THEN DASHES AWAY. LITTLE GENERAL WALKS TO THE SENTRY WHO HAS TURNED AND IS MARCHING BACK TOWARDS THE GATEWAY. THE SENTRY IS A BIT OF A WAG)

SENTRY:

'Struth! We got an invasion! 'Alt! Who goes there?

(THE LITTLE GENERAL COMES HAPPILY TO THE SENTRY AND STANDS BEFORE HIM, SMILING. THE SENTRY SEES THE NOTE PINNED TO THE LITTLE GENERAL'S SHIRT, AND SCREWS UP HIS EYES AT IT, PUZZLED)

SENTRY:

(CALLS) Oi! Corporal!

(THE CORPORAL COMES FROM THE GUARDHOUSE)

CORPORAL:
Hello.... hello.... It's the Little General.

SENTRY:
The what?

CORPORAL:
It's Woolie's kid. They call him the Little General on account of he looks like a little general.

SENTRY:
(TO THE GENERAL) What's this say, then?

CORPORAL:
(READS) "Please take me to Captain Woolcot".

SENTRY:
Think we ought to?

CORPORAL:
He's in the Officer's Mess, talkin' tactics. The polo match, you know.

SENTRY:
Oh?

CORPORAL:
Oh. Better wait a while. Can't barge in there.

SENTRY:
(GRINS) I never met a General before... (TO LITTLE GENERAL) Begging your pardon, sir.

(THE SENTRY SALUTES THE LITTLE GENERAL. THE CHILD RETURNS A CUTE SALUTE)

CORPORAL:

Oh, excuse me, sir, it's just come to me notice you aren't dressed proper for a General... Come with me. Hop up. Left, right, left, right. Now, you come with me.

(THE CORPORAL TAKES LITTLE GENERAL'S HAND AND LEADS HIM INTO THE GUARDHOUSE. THE SENTRY RESUMES HIS 'ON GUARD' POSITION. O.S. THE SOLDIERS LAUGH IN THE GUARDROOM)

SOLDIERS:

(O.S.) (UPROARIOUS LAUGHTER)

(THE SENTRY TRIES TO MAINTAIN HIS MILITARY DEMEANOUR)

SOLDIERS:

(O.S.) (MORE LAUGHTER)

CORPORAL:

(O.S.) Call out the Guard!!

(THE SOLDIERS EMERGE FROM THE GUARDHOUSE AND LINE UP. THE SENTRY JOINS THEM. THERE IS A MOMENT'S SILENCE, THEN THE CORPORAL COMES THROUGH THE DOOR HOLDING LITTLE GENERAL'S HAND. LITTLE GENERAL LOOKS HILARIOUS. HE HAS BEEN DRESSED IN AN OFFICER"S HAT AND A FULL DRESS COAT. A SWORD HAS BEEN STRAPPED TO HIS WAIST AND IT TRAILS LUDICROUSLY BEHIND HIM, WITH HIS COAT-TAILS)

CORPORAL:

Atten-shun! The Little General will now inspect the Regiment! Royal salute – present arms!!!
(O.S. THE BAND PLAYS. 'THE LITTLE GENERAL'S PARADE')

(THE LITTLE GENERAL MARCHES OUT TO FACE THE SOLDIERS. HE INSPECTS THE TROOPS. THE CORPORAL, EVERY NOW AND THEN, PAUSES TO STRAIGHTEN A COLLAR OR PUSH A BUTTON. SOON, THE SOLDIERS ARE READIED TO BE EVEN SILLIER)

CORPORAL:

(FOLLOWING) Now smarten up there, this is a very important occasion.

CORPORAL:

Squad present arms. (HE SALUTES LITTLE GENERAL, LITTLE GENERAL DOES THE SAME)

(IN A COMIC ROUTINE, THE CORPORAL AND LITTLE GENERAL TAKE THE SALUTE WHILE THE SOLDIERS MARCH COMICALLY, WHICH ENDS WITH THEM TOPPLING OVER LIKE A ROW OF TIN SOLDIERS.

UNBEKNOWNST TO THEM, COLONEL BRYANT AND CAPTAIN WOOLCOT, DRESSED IN THEIR POLO OUTFITS AND CARRYING POLO STICKS, HAVE APPEARED AND ARE WATCHING THE LAST MOMENTS OF THE PERFORMANCE, THUNDERSTRUCK. ESTHER IS WITH THEM. WHEN THE LITTLE GENERAL SEES ESTHER, HE RUNS HAPPILY TO HER.

THE SOLDIERS GRADUALLY BECOME AWARE OF
THE DISASTER AND SHEEPISHLY FORM
THEMSELVES INTO A RAGGED QUAKING LINE.
THE CORPORAL SALUTES COLONEL BRYANT,
WHO BARELY TOUCHES HIS CAP WITH HIS
RIDING CROP IN RESPONSE)

BRYANT:

Are these your men, Mr Woolcot?

WOOLCOT:

Yes, sir.

BRYANT:

Do you remember what the Iron Duke said to his troops,
Mr Woolcot?

WOOLCOT:

Yes, sir.

BRYANT:

Pray tell us, Mr Woolcot.

WOOLCOT:

He said, sir: I don't know what you men will do to the
enemy, but by God you terrify me.

BRYANT:

Thank you, Mr Woolcot. (TO MEN) Indeed you terrify all
of us. To think our future could be in your hands? Abooout
turn. (ONE TURNS THE WRONG WAY) Nincompoop!
No wonder the French and the Russians are on our
doorstep. You buffoon! Where do you think you are going?

SOLDIER:

I'm scared!

BRYANT:

You are a disgrace to your uniforms. Rabble! Rabble....
behaving like schoolboys. With soldiers like you, God help
Australia and the Empire. We may as well give in and
learn to eat snails. A twenty mile route march with full
pack, and four hours drill. See to it, Mr Woolcot.

WOOLCOT:

But Sir! (SOTTO) The polo match, sir?

BRYANT:

The polo match is cancelled Mr Woolcot! Discipline takes
precedence over polo!

WOOLCOT:

Yes, sir. (ASIDE, TO ESTHER) Esther go home, at once.
Inform Judith I shall see her on my return.

(ESTHER EXITS WITH LITTLE GENERAL)

(CAPTAIN WOOLCOT REJOINS THE ANGRY
COLONEL BRYANT)

BRYANT:

(TO THEM ALL) Discipline, men. Without it, we are lost!

(BLACKOUT)

(END OF SCENE)

ACT ONE   SCENE 6

BACK ON THE TRAM – LATE AFTERNOON

THE PROSCENIUM ARCH SIGN NOW READS,
'MUCH, MUCH LATER'.

(THE REAR PROJECTION TRACKS IN REVERSE TO
THE EARLIER JOURNEY.

THE TRAM IS AS BEFORE AND FOR THE MOST
PART REMAINS FIXED WHILST THE BACK CLOTH
PROJECTION COVERS THE JOURNEY BACK TO
SYDNEY. STREET LIGHTING HAS COMMENCED.

AT CAMPBELL PARADE LOOP [BONDI BEACH]
ALL THE YOUNG PEOPLE, INCLUDING THOSE
THAT ATTENDED FRENCH CLASS AND CAME TO
BONDI LATER, BOARD THE AGAIN NEARLY FULL
TRAM, NOW SET AT A REVERSE FOURTY FIVE
DEGREE ANGLE TO THE AUDIENCE.

PIP AND JUDY JOIN PASSENGERS IN ONE BAY
WHILE BUNTY, NELL, BABY AND MEG SQUEEZE
INTO THE CENTRE. ALDITH IS FORCED TO SIT
WITH BABY. THE OTHER YOUNG FOLK JAM INTO
ODD SPACES)

AT RISE:

THE SAME NEW AUSTRALIAN CONDUCTOR
STRUGGLES WITH THE NOISY YOUNG
PASSENGERS AS THEY HOLD UP THE TRAM,
BOARDING.

CONDUCTOR:

Hurr-y. Hurr-y. We caaan't be up-settin' the toiime -table. Hurr-y Miss.

(IN THE URGENCY ALDITH, LAST TO BOARD, IS SQUEEZED IN UNCOMFORTABLY NEXT TO BABY)

ALDITH:

Daaarling …

BABY:

Go away!

CONDUCTOR:

Fez pliz. Fez pliz. Neext stup Cuuur-lew-is Street.

(CONDUCTOR RINGS THE BELL. TRAM MOVES OFF AS DOES THE SCENIC PROJECTION)

JUDY:

Weren't the switchboard rides... (DREAMILY) heavenly.

PIP:

So heavenly, the first one made me sick. My heart's still in my mouth!

BUNTY:

Better than where you left what was in your stomach!

(THEY LAUGH – OTHER PASSENGERS REACT)

JUDY:

I wonder if Andrew has re-polished his shoes yet?

(ANDREW LOOKS DOWN AT HIS SHOES. ALL
HEADS NEARBY DO LIKEWISE)

JUDY:

(LOUDLY SO ALDITH HEARS) And did you see Aldith
McCarthy fall face first into the ice-cream cart?

PIP:

Actually, fizz, her love of ice-cream was not entirely …
her own. (HE GESTURES A PUSH)

(THEY LAUGH AGAIN WHILE ALDITH STEWS)

NELL:

Well, I liked the roller skates the best.

PIP:

But you couldn't stay upright.

NELL:

(ANNOYED) Yes, I could!

BUNTY:

Well, tell me then… why are your knees all black and
blue?

(NELL COVERS HER KNEES WITH HER DRESS)

BUNTY:

(GRUMPY AS USUAL) I wish we'd had some money.

MEG:

I wish we'd not gone. There's going to be a fearsome row.

CONDUCTOR:

(RINGING THE BELL) This stup.... Cuuur-lewis Street.

(THE TRAM STOPS. ONE PASSENGER ALIGHTS. THE CONDUCTOR RINGS THE BELL AND THE TRAM MOVES OFF)

ALDITH:

(MAKING CONVERSATION TO BABY) I saw you on the merry-go-round…oooooh la la? Was it fun?

BABY:

Go 'WAY, Aldiff!

ALDITH:

(CORRECTING HER WITH A SCORNFUL SMILE) Miss MacCarthy, Baby, dear.

MEG:

She's tired, Aldith. It's been a very long day …

BABY:

(PUT OUT AND STANDING UP TO ALDITH) AL-DIFF! You are a horrid OLD PIG, Aldiff MacCarfy, and I hate you…an' we all hate you…'cept Meg. An' Pip says you're a CREEP, and I wis' a drate big ziant would come and huff and puff an' blow you into ze middlest part of ze sea!

(THE PASSENGERS ALL REACT)

PIP:

Not much doubt about that!

MEG:

(TRYING TO COVER) She doesn't mean it, Aldith! She doesn't....

BABY:

I DO mean it!

(ALDITH IGNORS BABY AND ALTERS TACK. SHE PULLS HER DRESS IN HARD AT THE WAIST, DRAWING EVERYONE'S ATTENTION TO HER FIGURE. ALL SEE, PARTICULARLY THE YOUNG PEOPLE, AND THE CONDUCTOR WHO IS QUITE TAKEN ABACK AS HE PASSES, TURNING HIS HEAD AWAY IN EMBARRASSMENT)

CONDUCTOR:

This stup, Bond-i Junc-tion.

(THE TRAM STOPS. SEVERAL PASSENGERS ALIGHT. ALAN BOARDS, SEES MEG, WHO MOVES TO JOIN HIM AT THE BACK OF THE TRAM IN SPACE JUST VACATED WHERE THEY SIT TOGETHER. THE BELL RINGS AND THE TRAM MOVES OFF)

CONDUCTOR:

Next stup, Vic-too-ri-aa Baaa-rra-cks.

ALDITH:

(SPOKEN TO THE UNFORTUNATE ELDERLY LADY PASSENGER SEATED NEXT TO ALDITH BUT WHICH IS REALLY INTENDED FOR MEG'S EARS BEHIND) Did you know ... that true symmetrical grace can never be obtained with a waist more than twenty inches round. MY waist is only EIGHTEEN inches.

(MEG LOOKS VERY UNCOMFORTABLE AS SHE CHECKS HER WAIST. ALAN IS APPALLED)

LADY PASSENGER:
(VERY PROPER) I say … I do hope you thank our good Lord every night in your prayers.

GIRLS:
Ooh…aah.

BABY:
(SUDDENLY CONTINUING) An' I'm NOT tired!

(ALDITH REACTS FURIOUSLY. SHE CLIMBS DOWN ONTO THE RUNNING BOARD AND MOVES TO ANOTHER BAY ON THE TRAM)

ALDITH:
I have better things to do!

BABY:
(CALLING AFTER HER) I DO TH'O TOO!

LADY PASSENGER:
Good gracious.

(AT THE BACK OF THE TRAM)

ALAN:
(REFERRING TO ALDITH) All show! Take no notice of her! (HE CHANGES THE SUBJECT) But, this is a surprise. I've been studying with my tutor at his home. He makes himself available on Saturdays and it's too good an opportunity to pass up. Is this a regular Saturday journey?

MEG:

Well, no. We've been to 'French'. Well... sort of ...

ALAN:

I'm not sure I understand.

MEG:

Don't ask. Please... just don't ask.

ALAN:

If you wish. (HE LEANS TOWARD HER.
PASSENGERS DO THE SAME).... Perhaps I might see
you...from time to time?

MEG:

Perhaps...

ALAN:

I mean...that would be all right...wouldn't it?

MEG:

Perhaps...

ALAN:

and...would it be all right...if I...

MEG:

Yes, Mister Courtney?

ALAN:

Would it be all right...if I were to call you...Meg? That
would be all right...wouldn't it...(PAUSE) Miss Woolcot?

MEG:

(SHE CONSIDERS) That would be all right.

(PASSENGERS BEND AN EAR) But not in company…
not yet. All right?

ALAN:

(ELATED) All right? But not in company. (HE LOOKS
AT THE PASSENGERS, WHO LOOK AWAY) All right.

MEG:

(FORCEFULLY) All right…. (FED UP WITH THE
INTRUSION OF THE SURROUNDING PASSENGERS)
Sorry, I didn't mean that. (MORE GENTLY) All right,
Mister Courtney.

(WE DON'T HEAR ALAN AND MEG AS THEIR
CONVERSATION CONTINUES)

JUDY:

(TO PIP) You go home. I'll go back to the barracks and
pick up the General.

PIP:

Are you sure?

JUDY:

Yes. Look after the others, Pip. I'll catch the ferry after
yours. Don't worry.

CONDUCTOR:

This stup, Vic-too-ri-aa Baaa-rra-cks. All a-light for Vic-
too-ri-aa Baaa-rra-cks.

(THE TRAM STOPS AND JUDY CLIMBS QUICKLY
DOWN AND HEADS OFF, THE TRAM CLANGING
ITS BELL.)

IT IS GETTING DARK AND AS BEFORE, THE PHYSICAL TRAM NOW TRUCKS OFF [OPPOSITE DIRECTION TO SC 4] WHILE THE IMAGE OF THE WALLS AROUND VICTORIA BARRACKS REMAINS STILL, PROJECTED ON TO THE BACK CLOTH.

WITH THE TRAM GONE WE SEE STREET LIGHTS LIT IN THE TRAM SHELTER NOW FULL OF MOANING, WEARY, WORN-OUT SOLDIERS FROM WOOLCOT'S REGIMENT. THEY ARE COLLAPSED ON THE BENCH AND ON THE GROUND, LIKE DRUNKS.

JUDY DOES NOT SEE THEM. SHE STEPS DOWN AND HURRIES PAST ONE SIDE OF THE SHELTER. SHE HEARS A CONVERSATION)

SOLDIER ONE:
(POINTING AT THE TRAM) That one's too full. Maybe the next?

SOLDIER TWO:
(NEARLY FALLING OVER) Well, I need a rest.

SOLDIER ONE:
Did you see Woolie's face? It was red as fire!

SOLDIER TWO:
You should have seen YOURS when the Colonel arrived!

SOLDIER THREE:
Poor Woolie. That was one polo match he won't forget! And the Little General … wasn't he a hoot!

(JUDY REALISES WHO THEY ARE AND JUMPS FROM THE SHELTER WALL, FRIGHTENING THEM ALL)

JUDY:
(FURIOUS) That is my FATHER you are talking about! (THEY ALL GET TO THEIR FEET)

SOLDIER FOUR:
So sorry you should have heard us, Miss Woolcot. We meant no disrespect.

SOLDIER FIVE:
Our apologies, Ma'am. Fact is … we've only just finished four hour's drill. We're b.... (A HAND FROM BEHIND COVERS HIS MOUTH)

SOLDIER ONE:
None of us meant no harm, Miss Woolcot.

SOLDIERS ALL:
Hear, hear. Sorry, Miss.

SOLDIER TWO:
We've all took leave....

SOLDIER THREE:
to go t' 'ospidal.

SOLDIER FOUR:
Yeah. Th' Lord Nelson Brew'ry … Miller's Point. (THEY ALL LAUGH)

SOLDIER FIVE:
… far 'way from 'ere as possible.

JUDY:
> And where is my little brother?

SOLDIER TWO:
> Don't you know? Your mother, I mean Mrs Woolcot, took the little mite home. Orders of Captain Woolcot!

SOLDIER THREE:
> Polo match was aborted.

SOLDIER FOUR:
> Barracks lost by default.

JUDY:
> Oh dear.......

SOLDIER FIVE:
> If it's any consolation, Miss, it ain't been such a great day for us, neither.

> (JUDY RUNS OFF STAGE)

> (BLACKOUT)

> (END OF SCENE)

ACT ONE   SCENE SEVEN

WOOLCOT'S STUDY - SATURDAY NIGHT

AT RISE:
> (PIP, MEG, BUNTY,, NELL AND BABY ARE MARCHED ON STAGE BY WOOLCOT AND LINED AGAINST THE WALL. JUDY IS MISSING)

WOOLCOT:
Left, right, left, right, Halt!

(ESTHER FOLLOWS THEM IN, VERY ANXIOUS)

WOOLCOT:
(TO ESTHER) Has Judith arrived yet?

ESTHER:
Not yet. (THE FERRY WHISTLE SOUNDS IN THE DISTANCE) That's the ferry, now. (TURNING TO FACE HIM DIRECTLY) John … please don't do this.

WOOLCOT:
Don't? Are you serious? I intend to do it. I must.

ESTHER:
But …

WOOLCOT:
You were there. You saw it. I was made to look a fool in front of my own men. Made to look an incompetent.

ESTHER:
Don't I have any say?

WOOLCOT:
Not in this, Esther. What could you possibly say in their defence?

(A PAUSE. ESTHER IS UNABLE TO REPLY)

WOOLCOT:
They've been allowed to run wild. To do as they please. Someone must now enforce discipline around here.

ESTHER:

Are you blaming me... for what happened today?

WOOLCOT:

I prefer to talk of this at a more private time. I must ask you not to interfere.

(ESTHER EXITS AS A DISHEVILLED JUDY ENTERS THE ROOM. ESTHER'S LOOK AS THEY PASS MAKES CLEAR THAT THERE IS NOTHING SHE CAN DO TO HELP. JUDY FALLS INTO LINE)

JUDY:

Father.... I'm afraid I may have caused you some.... er ... inconvenience.

(WOOLCOT IGNORES HER, AND SUMMONS PIP WITH HIS CROOKED FINGER. PIP COMES NERVOUSLY FORWARD, READY TO ACCEPT HIS PUNISHMENT)

JUDY:

It was my fault. I talked him into it ... he didn't want to.

WOOLCOT:

Do you think I'm not aware of that? Don't worry, Miss.... I have something special in store for you ...

(WOOLCOT TAPS PIP WITH THE RIDING CROP, AND GESTURES FOR HIM TO MOVE TO THE OTHER SIDE OF THE ROOM. THEY GO OFF-STAGE, AND WE HEAR THE HARD WHACKS OF THE RIDING CROP)

BUNTY:

(SOTTO) How many will he get?

JUDY:

Six …

NELL:

That's four …

MEG:

Five …

BABY:

Six …

BUNTY:

Seven.... eight…

(HE LOOKS ACCUSINGLY AT JUDY)

JUDY:

He's never given more than six before.

MEG:

Nine, ten.

NELL:

Golly Moses.

BUNTY:

He'll have such a sore bum.

(PIP APPEARS, ACCOMPANIED BY WOOLCOT WHO
LIFTS HIS CHIN WITH THE RIDING CROP, THEN

POINTS TO THE LINE WHICH PIP REJOINS,
RUBBING HIS BOTTOM.
WOOLCOT PARADES UP AND DOWN BEFORE
THEM, AND THEN BECKONS JUDY OUT IN FRONT)

WOOLCOT:

In military strategy, where one plan fails, you try another.
Now, I have tried punishing you all, and this has failed.
Perhaps, dealing with the ringleader may prove more
successful. (HE USES HIS RIDING CROP TO LIFT
JUDY'S CHIN, AS HE STARES AT HER) Next Monday
you will leave this house. I am sending you away to
boarding school.... Miss Burton's Academy in the Blue
Mountains. And there you will apply yourself to the
acquisition of social graces.... and there you will remain,
until that unlikely objective has been achieved.

(THE SHOCKED CHILDREN ALL SPEAK AT ONCE)

MEG:

Oh Judy, no; that's awful!

PIP:

That's not fair at all. I was just as much to blame.

BUNTY:

Awww! Father!

BABY:

Plea'th don't th'end her; plea'th don't.

NELL:

Please, no.... father?

(WOOLCOT WHACKS HIS THIGH FOR SILENCE)

92

WOOLCOT:

Enough! That is my decision!

(WOOLCOT SWEEPS OUT OF THE ROOM AND SLAMS THE DOOR)

MEG:

Oh, Judy ... it's freezing in the mountains. The air's so cold. It'll bring back your cough.

JUDY:

I'll be fine, Meg. I won't use much air. I'll only breathe when it's absolutely necessary.

BUNTY:

He can't do this. Esther'll fix it. We'll ask Esther.

JUDY:

Stop! ... All this wailing and lamentation... I'm not going to my execution you know. (TO NELL, WHO IS ALMOST IN TEARS) Don't cry Nell. Look, tell you what... you may borrow my bed till I return. It's bigger than yours and you'll be able to fit all your dolls in it... and the bears. Now, that's good news, isn't it?

NELL:

May I?

JUDY:

Yes... but no tears!

PIP:

French won't be the same without you, Joods.

JUDY:

Poor old Marceau. He'll have to do some teaching, with me gone.

MEG:

I'll miss you on the tram.

JUDY:

What? Why?

MEG:

He'll be there.

JUDY:

Andrew Courtney? That clown?

MEG:

No. His brother, Alan.

JUDY:

Ahaa. So it's him, is it?

MEG:

Don't tease.

JUDY:

(KINDLY) Meg... Alan Courtney doesn't know that girls exist.... except in his medical books. He's never even looked at you.

MEG:

Well... he's looking now.

JUDY:

Wow. Like that, is it?

(MEG NODS, "YES")

JUDY:

Well, he has nice eyes.... but Andrew's the one you have to worry about. He really fancies you.... he keeps telling everyone.

MEG:

Ohhh … does he?

BUNTY:

Judy … I wish you weren't going.

JUDY:

You're jealous of me; that's what it is. All that mountain ozone.... posh debutantes for company. Goodness me! In no time at all, I'll be chock-full of social graces, you wait and see.

PIP:

You'll hate it.

JUDY:

(DETERMINEDLY) Nonsense.
(NELL & BABY TAKE JUDY'S ARMS, POSSESSIVELY)

JUDY:

What's this?

BABY:

We love you.

NELL:

We do. We don't care if you are wicked.

JUDY:

Bless you. Bless you one and all.... sentimental fools.

(SHE BLOWS HER NOSE)

JUDY:

Now cheer up, everybody. After all, Pip got ten of the best.

PIP:

Which reminds me, Meg… you know I've always said those romantic novels of yours were useless?

MEG:

Yes …?

(PIP PULLS ONE OF HER BOOKS FROM INSIDE THE SEAT OF HIS TROUSERS AND HANDS IT TO HER)

PIP:

Not completely useless.

(THE YOUNGER CHILDREN LAUGH. MEG IS STILL UPSET BY THE THOUGHT OF JUDY'S BANISHMENT. JUDY REALISES AND GIVES HER A BIG SISTERLY HUG)

JUDY:

Come on, Meg... cheer up.

MEG:

Everything's so awful.

(LIGHTS FADE)

(END OF SCENE)

ACT ONE   SCENE EIGHT

'MISRULE' INTERIOR - EARLY MORNING

(THE PROSCENIUM ARCH SIGN READS, 'NEXT MONDAY')

AT RISE:

LIGHTS UP ON FOYER. THE SPACE IS EMPTY, PIP AND THE GROOM ENTER FROM THE DOOR THAT ACCESSES THE BACK OF THE HOUSE CARRYING A CABIN TRUNK. MARTHA FOLLOWS WITH A BUNDLE OF JUDY'S FRESHLY IRONED CLOTHES, WHICH SHE STARTS TO PACK.

PIP AND THE GROOM EXIT. MARTHA PACKS.

MARTHA:
Put it down there, thank you. Thank you, love. (SNIFFS) Poor little pet. Even if she is the devil herself sometimes.

(OVERHEARING THIS, WOOLCOT EXITS THE MASTER BEDROOM ONTO THE WALK-WAY UPSTAIRS AND DESCENDS THE STAIRCASE. MARTHA IS IN NO MOOD TO REACT. ESTHER FOLLOWS WOOLCOT. THEY HAVE CLEARLY BEEN ARGUING)

ESTHER:
John...

WOOLCOT:
No.

ESTHER:

I'm going to speak my mind, even if you don't wish to hear. (AWARE OF MARTHA WATCHING AND LISTENING) I'll attend to the rest of that, Martha.

MARTHA:

Yes, Madam. Poor little pet.

(SHE EXITS TO THE BACK OF THE HOUSE, WITH A REBELLIOUS LOOK AT THE CAPTAIN, WHICH SHE FULLY INTENDS HIM TO SEE. WOOLCOT SIGHS)

WOOLCOT:

Is everyone against me?

ESTHER:

In this matter, yes.

WOOLCOT:

What am I ... an ogre? ... a monster? Has it never occurred to you that what I am doing is for her own good? That as her father, I have my daughter's best interests at heart.

ESTHER:

You don't really believe that.

WOOLCOT:

I'll tell you what I believe. That the longer we countenance her irresponsible behaviour, the more difficult it will be for her to gain acceptance in polite society.

ESTHER:

Perhaps she doesn't want to gain acceptance in polite society?

WOOLCOT:

What, that's nonsense.

ESTHER:

Is it? You told me, one of the last things her mother said was, "Look after Judy, she's special". How will sending her away foster anything special in her? She needs her family about her.... and they need her. To banish her like this, for some silly misdemeanour, is capricious and cruel. You wrong yourself, as much as you wrong her. And it is not the action of a good father.

WOOLCOT:

How dare you tell me what it is to be a good father! Barely a woman, with all your now, twenty-four years experience.

ESTHER:

Sometimes, I'm not sure I know you, Mister Woolcot…

WOOLCOT:

Do you think this is easy? Why can't you understand that I have responsibilities. There has to be some discipline in this house!

ESTHER:

(APPEALING TO HIM) But not in this way. You try so hard… but this is not the way. Especially with Judy. "Such a free spirit… don't let her be shipwrecked on rocks the others will never come to."

WOOLCOT:

(SUDDENLY FURIOUS) Please do not quote my first wife to me. I am well aware of all within my purview of responsibility.

ESTHER:

> Well, Mister! That may be. But what this just burgeoning
> woman has to say to you now is between you and me!

> (SHE STANDS AT THE FOOT OF THE STAIRS,
> TURNS TO FACE HIM BELOW HER, PAUSES
> BRIEFLY, AND GATHERS HERSELF FOR WHAT
> SHE IS ABOUT TO SAY)

ESTHER:

> What, exactly ... is a woman to you?
> Is it someone not too old
> One, not very bold
> Someone flaunting top to derriere?
>
> Or is it someone with a heart
> Albeit not too smart
> But someone who's in love with you?
>
> Do you live your life alone?
> A distant man of stone
> Unreachable, untouchable,
> A fortress for a crutch to pull
> the wool over the eyes of all
> who seek to know you?
>
> What is this woman to you?
>
> This woman you would share,
> does she have a mind, rate a care?
> This pretty face to others you do show!
>
> .... and the heart that beats inside....
> can that heart in his wife confide?
> Does this woman count at all?

100

Well... go! Take the easy way.
Don't reveal yourself,
Don't expose yourself?
Lest all will know John Woolcot
and the man behind that pride!
.... and the feelings (SHE STARTS TO BREAK DOWN)
he must hide...

(HE BEGINS TO MOVE TOWARDS HER, HESITATES,
REALISING HE CAN'T CONSOLE HER)

(SHE RECOVERS AND CONTINUES IN A MORE
CONSIDERED TONE)

No! Go and hide the truth from all who care,
for there's no shame if your love you wear
on a sleeve, the same from which you wipe a tear
(BREAKS AGAIN)
in that way of love, not the way of fear …

Oh... what is this woman … to you?

(WOOLCOT LOOKS A BROKEN MAN LOOKS HARD
AT ESTHER, WHO GAZES BACK AT HIM,
UNREPENTANT. THERE IS A SIGNIFICANT PAUSE.
HE TAKES OUT HIS FOB WATCH AND GLANCES
AT IT)

WOOLCOT:
The carriage will be leaving in five minutes.

(HE EXITS TO THE BACK OF THE HOUSE. ESTHER
WIPES HER EYES AND CONTINUES TO PACK.
JUDY, FOLLOWED BY THE SUBDUED CHILDREN,
EXITS HER BEDROOM OFF THE UPSTAIRS WALK-

WAY. SHE IS SENSIBLY AND DRABLY DRESSED
FOR THE JOURNEY, IN CLOTHES COMPLETELY
DIFFERENT TO HER USUAL OUTLANDISH WEAR.
SHE DESCENDS THE STAIRS AS IF IT IS HER
EXECUTION.

JUDY CARRIES A SMALL TRAVEL BAG, AND A
MULTI-COLOURED CERAMIC POT. SHE PUTS
DOWN THE BAG AND FERRETS IN THE POT,
BRINGING OUT SMALL SCROLLS ALL TIED WITH
RIBBON AND NAME-TAGGED)

JUDY:

Original literature. Get your poems here. While they last,
ladies and gentlemen, specially written farewell poetry.

(SHE STARTS TO HAND OUT THE SCROLLS)

JUDY:

There's one for you, Little General… with small words and
big pictures. There's one for Baby, with animals and birds
in it and one for you Nell, with angels in it.

BABY & NELL:

(TOGETHER) Thank you, Judy.

JUDY:

Bunty, you'll never guess what your poem's about.

BUNTY:

Chocolate pudding?

JUDY:

No.... it's about.... it's about how much I'll miss you - even
if you are a piggy.

(JUDY AFFECTIONATELY PUSHES THE TIP OF BUNTY'S NOSE)

BUNTY:

Thanks Joods.

(JUDY'S FALSE HIGH SPIRITS ARE BECOMING MORE DIFFICULT TO SUSTAIN. ESTHER COMES IN WITH MORE IRONED AND FOLDED CLOTHES. SHE PACKS THEM. JUDY HANDS THE LAST TWO SCROLLS TO PIP AND MEG)

JUDY:

Pip… Meg… yours are full of sombre,… sentiment and sound advice about how to stay out of trouble.

(MEG TAKES JUDY'S HAND)

MEG:

Judy ….

PIP:

Thanks, sis.

(IN THE BACKGROUND, NELL AND BABY ARE TAKING TIME IN ELABORATELY GIFT-WRAPPING THEIR FAREWELL PRESENTS TO JUDY. ESTHER KNEELS TO TIDY THE TRAVEL BAG)

ESTHER:

(SHOWING JUDY A SANDWICH PACK AS SHE PUTS IT INTO HER TRAVEL BAG) For the journey. (ESTHER'S HAND TOUCHES SOMETHING) Good heavens! (SHE TAKES OUT A LARGE, DANGEROUS-

LOOKING SHANGHAI) Is this absolutely essential for life in a boarding school?

JUDY:

It's Bunty's "goodbye" present. It was either that or Algenon the frog.

BUNTY:

It's my best one. It's for emergencies.

JUDY:

…. and Meg gave me a bracelet and Pip gave me a pen for writing lots of letters home with, and Little General gave me a rock.

ESTHER:

That's handy.

(JUDY HOLDS UP THE ROCK)

JUDY:

Ah, but it's not an ordinary rock, it's special. It has a face on it.... well, sort of.... I'm taking it for luck. I might need a bit of luck.

(SHE IS ALMOST AT BREAKING POINT. ESTHER TRIES TO PUT AN ARM AROUND HER. JUDY EVADES IT)

ESTHER:

Dear Judy. It's not forever ….

JUDY:

It nearly is.

104

NELL:

> We're ready now, Judy.

BABY:

> We got th'or prethents.

> (AT THAT MOMENT, WOOLCOT RE-ENTERS FROM THE BACK OF THE HOUSE, FOLLOWED BY THE GROOM CARRYING A LEATHER CASE ON HIS SHOULDER. NELL AND BABY SHRINK BACK, THEIR PRESENTS FORGOTTEN. ESTHER CLOSES THE TRUNK)

WOOLCOT:

> (TO GROOM) Take them to the carriage. Come along.

> (THE SQUEAKING FRONT DOOR IS PARTICULARLY NOTICEABLE AS WOOLCOT OPENS IT, STANDING INSIDE FOR THE GROOM TO EXIT WITH THE TRUNK. JUDY IS DETERMINED NOT TO LET HIM SEE SHE IS NEARLY IN TEARS. WOOLCOT APPEARS STRAINED AND TENSE. JUDY TAKES HER CRYSTAL RAINBOW MAKER, TWISTING IT IN HER HANDS)

WOOLCOT:

> (IN THE SILENCE) What's wrong with you all?

ESTHER:

> I'm sure you know what's wrong.

MEG:

> (BURSTS OUT) Father, please let her stay.

PIP:

It'll never happen again. On my honour, I won't let her do anything foolish again.

BUNTY:

Bet she's perfect now.

NELL:

She'll be good, you'll see.

BUNTY:

She belongs here...

NELL:

... with us. She's in our family ...

BABY:

.... no-vun elth-eth....

WOOLCOT:

Stop this nonsense. I think you're all demented! She's going to a perfectly good school. I've paid a quarter in advance already, and I can assure you good people it's not going to waste.

PIP:

Judy, don't just stand there. Ask him yourself. Go on.... ask him.

(A LONG TENSE SILENCE. JUDY MOVES TO HIM)

JUDY:

Father, please may I stay?

106

(TAKEN OFF-GUARD, HE STEPS BACK AWAY
FROM HER, AND THE SUDDEN MOVEMENT
KNOCKS THE GLASS PRISM FROM JUDY'S HAND.
IT DROPS AND SMASHES TO THE FLOOR.

ALL THE CHILDREN REACT. MEG STOOPS AND
GATHERS UP THE PIECES.

JUDY JUST GAZES STRAIGHT AHEAD. WOOLCOT
IS SHAKEN AND SORRY, BUT UNABLE TO FULLY
EXPRESS IT)

WOOLCOT:
What was that?

BUNTY:
Her rainbow maker.

JUDY:
It was.... nothing important.

WOOLCOT:
No, I am sorry … you may not stay. Don't be long. The
carriage is waiting.

(WOOLCOT EXITS THE BACK OF HOUSE DOOR.
MEG SADLY OFFERS JUDY THE REMNANTS OF
HER 'RAINBOW MAKER'. SHE SHAKES HER HEAD)

(NELL TUGS AT HER CLOTHES TO ATTRACT
ATTENTION)

NELL:
Judy... (SHE HANDS OVER HER WRAPPED

PRESENT) It's a book with no pictures, especially for grown-ups, 'cos you're one.... sort of....

JUDY:

Thank you, Nell. (SHE KNEELS AND KISSES HER)

NELL:

You have to read it on the train.

JUDY:

I will.

(BABY HOLDS UP HER PRESENT, MUTELY)

JUDY:

For me?

BABY:

She's for company. Her name is Joan Sleeper, and she's only broken a little bit.

JUDY:

She's wonderful. (JUDY HUGS HER) I'll talk to her every night.

(ESTHER HAS BEEN WATCHING THIS. NOW SHE COMES FORWARD)

ESTHER:

Judy, I can give you nothing... but my fondest love.

(ESTHER GIVES HER A LONG HUG. JUDY MAKES HER FAREWELLS. AT THE END OF IT, ESTHER HUGS JUDY ONE MORE TIME)

(WOOLCOT ENTERS, STANDING JUST INSIDE THE FRONT DOOR)

WOOLCOT:

Hurry now or she'll miss her train!

(THE GROOM RE-ENTERS FROM OUTSIDE, UP THE STEPS FROM BELOW STAGE TO THE STILL OPEN IMAGINARY FRONT DOOR . HE STANDS FORMALLY, JUST INSIDE, WAITING. JUDY, IN HER STIFF AND FORMAL CLOTHES, INCONGRUOUSLY HOLDS THE BATTERED DOLL, MOVES TO WOOLCOT AND GRAVELY HOLDS OUT HER HAND FOR HER FATHER TO SHAKE.

HE STARES BLANKLY, UNABLE TO MAKE THE GESTURE OF RECONCILIATION. JUDY DROPS HER HAND, TURNS AND QUICKLY EXITS, ALMOST SAYING GOODBYE TO 'MISRULE' AS SHE LEAVES, FOLLOWED BY THE GROOM AT A RESPECTFUL DISTANCE. THE FAMILY MINUS WOOLCOT FOLLOW FROM A DISTANCE, EXITING INTO THE PIT BELOW AS WOOLCOT IS LEFT ALONE ON THE STAGE, DEEPLY UPSET, ALMOST CALLING HER BACK. THE DEATHLY SILENCE SHATTERS AS HE CLOSES THE DOOR, SQUEAKING LOUDER THAN EVER BEFORE. THE FINAL CLICK AS IT LOCKS SHUT IS OMINOUS. WOOLCOT REMAINS ALONE AND REMOTE.)

(THE LIGHTS FADE AS THE DARKNESS BECOMES DRAMATIC. DURING THIS THE SET CLEARS)

(END OF SCENE)

ACT ONE   SCENE NINE

BARE STAGE – LIGHTS DIMMED

(AN EERIE HALF-LIGHT EMERGES. A DRUM ROLL AND SHORT MILITARY DRUM FIGURE ACCOMPANIES FOUR MEN [STAGEHANDS] IN OMINOUS BLACK AS THEY MARCH OUT BACK STAGE PROMPT DIAGONALLY IN A LINE TO FRONT STAGE OFF PROMPT. THEY FORM INTO TWO LINES OF TWO, ABOUT TURN, STAND TO ATTENTION AS TWO HORSE CLADDING FORMATIONS DROP FROM THE GRID TO FALL OVER THE TWO LINES TURNING THEM INTO TWO HORSES STANDING SIDE BY SIDE POINTING BACK UPSTAGE FROM WHERE THEY HAVE COME. THE SHAFTS BELONGING TO THE DOGCART WAITING IN THE WINGS ARE PART OF THE HORSE CLADDING.

THE WHIP CRACKS OFF STAGE. THE TWO HORSES START TO CLIP -CLOP SIDE BY SIDE TOWARD THEIR DESTINATION. THE SOUNDS OF THE HORSES, THE CLATTERING WHEELS OF THE DOGCART AND THE CRACKS OF THE WHIP MAKE UP THE DRAMATIC SFX. THE DOGCART CONTAINING THE DEPRESSED JUDY AND DRIVEN BY THE GROOMSMAN WHO HOLDS THE REINS COMES INTO VIEW. BEHIND, STANDS THE FAMILY WAVING SLOWLY, MINUS WOOLCOT, THEIR HEADS BOWED, THE CHILDREN CRYING AS THE DOGCART MOVES DIAGONALLY ACROSS AND OFF THE STAGE. JUDY DOES NOT LOOK BACK, DOES NOT RETURN THE FAMILY'S WAVE. THE DOGCART DISAPPEARS INTO THE

110

BACKSTAGE WINGS AND THE FAMILY ARE LEFT
CLINGING TOGETHER AS LIGHTS GENTLY FADE
AND THE CURTAIN COMES DOWN)

(END OF SCENE)

ACT ONE   SCENE TEN

MISS BURTON'S ACADEMY FOR GIRLS IN THE BLUE MOUNTAINS.

SEVERAL MONTHS LATER. DAYTIME.

(THE SIGN ON THE PROSCENIUM ARCH READS,
'SEVERAL MONTHS LATER')

SFX OF NATIVE BIRDS SOUND, KOOKABURRAS,
MAGPIES ETC. A LARGE SCHOOLROOM WITH A
VIEW OF SANDSTONE-CLIFFED MOUNTAINS. THE
"THREE SISTERS" ARE SEEN THROUGH A HUGE
PICTURE WINDOW, OUTSIDE OF WHICH IS A
LEDGE ON WHICH SIT A FLOCK OF RESIDENT
GALAHS.

INSIDE, THERE IS A SET OF WHITE STEPS,
PYRAMID IN FORM, USED FOR PRACTISING
WALKING-UP-STAIRS-IN-A-LADYLIKE-MANNER.
A WHITE DUMMY DOOR IN A FRAME, FOR
PRACTISING ENTERING-A-ROOM-CORRECTLY.
THERE IS A PIANO TO ONE SIDE, AT WHICH MISS
JOLLY, AN ELDERLY TEACHER, PEERS
MYOPICALLY THROUGH A PINCE-NEZ AS SHE
PLAYS THE MELODY OF "DEPORTMENT".

AT RISE:

MISS JOLLY STOPS AS MISS BURTON ENTERS
BRISKLY' PICKS UP HER CANE AND TAPS FOR
ATTENTION ON THE PIANO.

MISS JOLLY:
Ah, Miss Burton.

MISS BURTON:
Miss Jolly. Are we ready?

MISS JOLLY:
Yes, Miss Burton.

MISS BURTON:
Don't forget now. It's the deportment lesson, dear.

MISS JOLLY:
It's been the deportment lesson every Thursday afternoon
for twenty-five years, Miss Burton.

MISS BURTON:
Well, one is getting on, you know. One doesn't get any
younger, and …

MISS JOLLY:
Undeniably, Miss Burton, but because one is old, does not
mean one is stupid. Carry on.

MISS BURTON:
Er... yes... yes.

(THROUGH THE LARGE PICTURE WINDOW WE
SEE THE GALAHS WATCHING AND SQWARKING

[ALMOST AT THE POMPOUS MISS BURTON]. MISS JOLLY BEGINS TO PLAY AS MISS BURTON MOVES TO CALL INTO THE WINGS)

MISS BURTON:

Gels! Gels! Straight line please. Deep breathing now. That's it.

(SHE SNAPS HER FINGERS LIKE A CIRCUS TRAINER. MISS BURTON STARTS TO WALK BACKWARDS, STIFFLY, AS SHE IS FOLLOWED BY A CROCODILE OF SCHOOLGIRLS OF ALL SHAPES AND SIZES. THEY WALK SLOWLY AND STIFFLY, WITH PRECISE, METICULOUS MOVEMENTS LIKE A SET OF CLOCKWORK DOLLS, KEEPING PERFECT TIME TO THE MUSIC.

SEVERAL SEQUENCES ARE CALLED OUT BY MISS BURTON, INCLUDING 'CHINS HELD HIGH', 'BACKS STRAIGHT', 'HOW TO CROSS LEGS APPROPRIATELY', DECORUM IN POLITE SOCIETY', 'KEEPING KNEES TOGETHER' ETC.
SEPERATING THESE OFTEN COMIC SEQUENCES IN WHICH JUDY MISBEHAVES APALLINGLY, THE ACTION IS FROZEN AT VARIOUS MOMENTS, AS THE CENTRE STAGE DARKENS AND A SPOTLIGHT PICKS OUT SPEAKERS IN TURN.

FIRST, PIP APPEARS IN A POOL OF LIGHT)

PIP:

Dear Judy,
How is life at boarding school?
Things are rotten at "Misrule".
I'm in the local cricket team... they let me

play at slip.
And that's about my news for now.
Your loving brother, Pip.

P.S. Do you think we'll beat the Poms when they bring
their team out here next year?

(PIP DISAPPEARS. ACTION RETURNS AS THE
DEPORTMENT CLASS RESUMES, THEN SUSPENDS
AGAIN)

(THE SPOT LIGHTS UP AND MEG APPEARS)

MEG:

Dear Judy,
Life is a tragedy.
I don't know who said that, but I'm sure someone did.
Everyone misses you. Your loving sister, Meg.

(MEG DISAPPEARS. DEPORTMENT CLASS ACTION
RETURNS, ONLY TO SUSPEND AGAIN. BUNTY,
NELL, BABY, THE GENERAL AND ESTHER APPEAR
IN A POOL OF LIGHT)

BUNTY:

Dear Judy,
Baby has a toothache,

NELL:

Bunty has the flu,
The General's lost a tooth,

BABY:

And Nell's new frock is blue.

114

BUNTY:

And dear, darling Judy
We all miss you.

ESTHER:

Dear Judy,
We so very badly need you here
to make us all laugh again.
All my love, Esther.

(THEY DISAPPEAR. THE SPOTLIGHT CUTS AND
THE LESSON AGAIN RESUMES. THE CLASS
FREEZES AGAIN AS WOOLCOT APPEARS IN A
SPOTLIGHT, FROWNING OVER A LETTER HE HAS
WRITTEN, AND HOLDING A SMALL POSTAL
PACKAGE, UNSEALED)

WOOLCOT:

Dear Judith… Judy.... (CLEARS HIS THROAT)… I
enclose one of those glass prism objects, which was
unfortunately broken on the day of your departure.
(HE TAKES IT FROM HIS POCKET, LOOKS AT IT
FOR A MOMENT, THEN PLACES IT IN THE
PACKAGE. HE RESUMES READING HIS LETTER)

WOOLCOT:

I hope and trust you are behaving, and learning decorum....
and.... er.... other attributes.... which will stand you in good
stead in the years ahead.
Your affectionate father... John R. B. Woolcot.

(WOOLCOT DISAPPEARS AS THE CLASS PERFORM
LIKE OBEDIENT ZOMBIES, THIS TIME CARRYING
BOOKS ON THEIR HEADS TO WALK ERECTLY.

JUDY SUDDENLY REBELS. THE BOOKS FLY EVERYWHERE)

(MISS JOLLY KEEPS PLAYING THE PIANO)

MISS BURTON:
Miss Jolly … Miss Jolly! Stop!

(MISS JOLLY STOPS. THERE COMES A FINAL BLAST OF HORRIFIC SQWARKS FROM THE RESIDENT GALAHS)

MISS BURTON:
(SPOKEN) Judith Woolcot, how long have you been with us now?

JUDY:
Three years.

MISS BURTON:
Don't be ridiculous. It's been three months.

JUDY:
Well, it seems like three years.

GIRLS:
(GIGGLE)

MISS BURTON:
Silence.

JUDY:
Actually, it's eighty-one days, seven hours, and twenty-four minutes.

MISS BURTON:

And not once have you behaved satisfactorily. Your presence is a disturbing influence on the other gels. You have been disobedient, provocative, perverse and insolent. You are a disgrace to your family, and to this school.

JUDY:

There's no need to beat about the bush, Miss Burton. If you don't like me, say so.

GIRLS:

(GIGGLE & SNIGGER)

MISS BURTON:

(FURIOUS) Stop it! (TO THEM) You will all go to your rooms and write out fifty times: "I must not laugh at silly obnoxious gels." Go! Go!

(THE GIRLS ALL EXIT, WITH DARK LOOKS AT JUDY FOR CAUSING THIS)

MISS BURTON:

(TO JUDY) And you! You will go without afternoon tea and supper, and you will report to the discipline mistress, at once.

JUDY:

No.

(MISS JOLLY GASPS)

MISS BURTON:

(APOPLECTIC) What did you say?

JUDY:

N – O Spells No!

(MISS BURTON POKES AT HER WITH THE LONG
CANE. JUDY GRABS IT AND RIPS IT FROM HER.
NOW SHE POKES AT MISS BURTON, PUSHING HER
OFFSTAGE. JUDY TOSSES THE CANE BEHIND HER)

(THERE IS A PAUSE. FINALLY, MISS JOLLY
RECOVERS ENOUGH TO CLEAR HER THROAT.
JUDY LAUGHS AND TURNS TO THE FASCINATED
AND STARTLED MISS JOLLY)

JUDY:

I do it on purpose, Miss Jolly.

MISS JOLLY:

I can see that, dear.

JUDY:

It gingers up the lessons a bit.

MISS JOLLY:

It gingered up this one.

JUDY:

Deportment. This place is like a wife factory… supplying
brood mares for graziers, lawyers and businessmen.

MISS JOLLY:

I've not heard it expressed quite like that, but it's true.... our
graduates generally er.... marry well.

JUDY:

Doesn't say much for the husbands. (SHE PICKS UP A
BOOK) Look at this, "The Perfect Lady." A lady does this.
A lady does that. A lady says "Frarnce"... a lady has "arnts
in her parnts."

(MISS JOLLY CHUCKLES)

JUDY:

(POMPOUS VOICE) And Young Judith, what did they
teach you at Miss Burton's Academy? Ehh? Ehhh?
Philosophy? Geometry? (IRISH) Oh no, sir... I learned to
walk with a book on me head, and sit down like an arthritic
duck.

MISS JOLLY:

(CHUCKLES) You're irrepressible, Judy.

(JUDY SMILES. SHE GOES TO THE WINDOW AND
LOOKS OUT, TAKING THE NEW CRYSTAL FROM
HER POCKET, HOLDING IT UP TO THE BRIGHT
LIGHT AND WATCHING THE COLOURS)

MISS JOLLY:

What's that?

JUDY:

My rainbow maker... given to me by my father. See?
Light goes in; colour comes out.

MISS JOLLY:

Ah, yes.

JUDY:

My brother Pip.... crushingly academic and literal minded, says it's something to do with physics. But I know it's to do with magic.

(MISS JOLLY SMILES, LIKING HER. JUDY TOSSES THE CRYSTAL IN THE AIR, CATCHES IT AND POCKETS IT)

JUDY:

I feel like doing something romantic and daring.

MISS JOLLY:

Do you, dear?

JUDY:

Yes, some escapade that will cause consternation and bewilderment throughout the entire civilized world.... and one or two heathen countries as well ...

MISS JOLLY:

That's nice, dear.

JUDY:

I'm always thinking about such things. Why don't you do something romantic and daring?

MISS JOLLY:

Me? Good gracious! What do you have in mind?

JUDY:

Become a bushranger.... or a pirate. Or we could start our own foreign Legion - women only.

MISS JOLLY:

Or run away to sea.

JUDY:

Or.... to anywhere …

MISS JOLLY:

I could run away to Moonee Ponds.

JUDY:

Is that romantic and daring?

MISS JOLLY:

Oh yes, very. My married sister lives there. She's been asking me for years to come and stay with her … but I've never been brave enough to leave here.

JUDY:

What will Miss Burton do to me?

MISS JOLLY:

I really don't know. Nothing like this has ever happened before.

JUDY:

Or... probably... will ever happen again. One thing I know, there'll be nothing to eat tonight.

(BLACKOUT)

(END OF SCENE)

ACT ONE   SCENE ELEVEN

'MISRULE' – INTERIOR – EARLY MORNING

AT RISE:

MEG SNEAKS INTO THE HALLWAY EXITING THE
KITCHEN DOOR, CHECKING SHE IS NOT SEEN, AS
SHE TIP TOES CARRYING A BUNDLE OF ITEMS
INCLUDING FRUIT, A BUCKET, SOAP, TOWELS
ETC. TO SFX SHE CHECKS AGAIN THAT SHE IS
NOT SEEN AND QUICKLY DISAPPEARS OUT THE
FRONT DOOR THAT SQUEAKS AS USUAL,
CLOSING IT BEHIND HER. A PAUSE, THEN PIP, IN
HIS GRAMMAR SCHOOL UNIFORM, DOES THE
SAME, CARRYING BREAD, BUTTER AND A LEG OF
LAMB.

MARTHA EXITS THE NURSERY WHERE BABY AND
NELL SIT WITH THE GENERAL, EATING. SHE
TURNS ON THE LIGHTS IN THE FOYER AND
ENTERS THE KITCHEN, SOON EXITING,
PERPLEXED, BACK TO THE FOYER, SCRATCHING
HER HEAD) Where's that leg of lamb gone?.... only
carved it this morning. I'm sure I did that. I'm sure… going
mad …

(TURNING TO GO UP THE STAIRCASE SHE
COLLIDES DRAMATICALLY WITH BUNTY,
TRYING NOT TO BE SEEN, AS HE PASSES THE
FOOT OF THE STAIRS ON HIS WAY OUT FROM THE
DOOR LEADING TO THE REAR OF THE HOUSE.
BUNTY CARRIES A LARGE ROLLED UP RUG
BULGING WITH ITEMS. CHECKING CAREFULLY
WITH EACH STEP THAT NO-ONE SEES HIM, HE

DROPS THE LOT AS HE GETS THE SHOCK OF HIS
LIFE)

MARTHA:

Bunty? What are you doing?

BUNTY:

Ahhhh!! Ooooh…cripes? Ooooh…t'wasn't me. It's not my
fault.

MARTHA:

What's not your fault, THIS time. And what's inside that
rug?

(MARTHA OPENS THE RUG TO REVEAL A
CHICKEN LEG, CAKE, APPLES AND ORANGES AND
A DECANTER OF WINE…AND THE MAIL)

BUNTY:

Nothing…nothing...

MARTHA:

Why are you stealing things, Bunty? (PICKING UP EACH
ITEM) Wine? What POSSIBLE use could you have for
WINE? And the family's best crystal decanter, too. It could
have been broken! …and just WHAT… are you doing with
the mail? (A PAUSE) Your father will have to be told.

BUNTY:

No. No. Please no, Martha. (HE CUPS HIS HAND TO
TELL HER SOMETHING SECRETLY. MARTHA
BENDS DOWN AS HE WHISPERS SOMETHING TO
MARTHA)

NELL:

(ON HEARING THE HEAVILY PRONOUNCED WORD 'MAIL' NELL GIVES AN EXCITED SHOUT) Has the postman been? (RUSHING OUT OF THE NURSERY SHE SEES THE LETTERS ON THE FLOOR, PICKS UP THE PILE, TAKING THEM TO THE SMALL DESK AT THE FOOT OF THE STAIRCASE. SHE LOOKS AT THE LETTERS AND LIFTS THE TOP ONE) Yeaaah! It's from Judy! A letter from Judy...

(HER EXCITEMENT IS HEARD BY ESTHER AND WOOLCOT WHO SUDDENLY APPEAR FROM THE REAR OF THE HOUSE)

NELL:

(LOOKING AT THE ENVELOPE) ...it's HER writing!

(WOOLCOT, ESTHER BEHIND HIM, REACHES NELL. BUNTY IS UNSEEN BY THEM AS HE INDICATES FRANTICALLY TO MARTHA TO PLEASE NOT TELL WOOLCOT)

WOOLCOT:

(UNABLE TO SEE THE RUG ON THE FLOOR) What's that, Nellie?

(HE BECKONS TO HER AND NELL PASSES THE PILE OF LETTERS TO HIM, JUDY'S ON TOP)

NELL:

It's a letter, father. I think it's from Judy.

WOOLCOT:

(EXAMINING IT) It is. It is indeed.

NELL:

It's not addressed to you.

(HE SMILES AT HER, PUTS THE OTHER LETTERS
DOWN ON THE DESK, AND OPENS JUDY'S LETTER
EXCITEDLY. HE READS TO HIMSELF WHILE THE
OTHERS WAIT IN SILENCE. AS HE READS, HIS
EXPRESSION CHANGES FROM JOY TO PAIN)

NELL:

What's she say, father? What's her news?

(WOOLCOT DOES NOT ANSWER. THERE IS A LONG
PAUSE. HE STARES INTO SPACE, CLEARLY
DISTRESSED)

ESTHER:

John…is something wrong?

(WOOLCOT HANDS ESTHER JUDY'S LETTER.
ESTHER READS AND IS SHOCKED AND THEN
SADDENED. SHE THEN READS ALOUD)

ESTHER:

Dear All,
Your letters make me cry. Life is wonderful.
I have only had five beatings…which is not too bad. The
food is 'yuk'…cold slop for breakfast, warm slop for
lunch…, and no slop for tea…on account of me being sent
to my room…most nights anyway. I'm not always so
lucky.

Father is right about 'finishing' school. This place is sure
designed to 'finish' one. Is that what he had in mind for
me?

To Pip…you would love the girls. They will make perfect wives. You can be sure and certain they will always do as they're told. Probably ask permission to die…when the time comes.

To Meg…this would be a wonderful place for Aldith…she'd love the mental stimulation.

To Bunty…no cream buns here…except on Miss Burton's neck.

To Nell and Baby…do you remember the line of galahs above the verandah at Yarrahappini? Well they are all here now, lined up outside…they come every morning…first thing.

To General…do you remember that very swish military band… the day of your inspection at father's barracks? Well here there's a one woman band…called Miss Jolly…very un-swish at the pianoforte…I bet if you inspected her…she'd fail.

To Esther…I don't suppose Father wants to hear from me… but somehow…in your very special way…that only you know how…would you please convey to him the concept…. that I still love him…very much.

(WOOLCOT JUST STANDS LOOKING INTO SPACE, SAYING NOTHING. A TEAR DEVELOPS. HE COVERS HIS FACE WITH BOTH HANDS IN DISTRESS. THE OTHERS ALL LOOK AT HIM AND THEN LOOK AWAY AS HE TRIES TO HIDE HIS EMBARRASSMENT)

WOOLCOT:

(SLOWLY AND QUIETLY) I think I am going to pay Miss Burton a visit.

(MARTHA AND BUNTY ARE NOW IN THE OPEN AS ESTHER CONTINUES READING)

ESTHER:

To all…I am missing you…more than I can say…in a letter…

(ESTHER BURSTS INTO TEARS. WOOLCOT COMFORTS HER BUT SHE ONLY HALF RECEIVES HIM. HE PICKS UP THE REMAINING LETTERS AND BEGINS SORTING THROUGH THEM FOR A DIVERSION AS MARTHA, HOLDING BUNTY'S HAND, STEPS TOWARD HIM)

MARTHA:

(TO BUNTY) Your father must be told.

(THE BROKEN DOOR BELL JANGLES SHARPLY. MARTHA REACTS STARTLED, THEN STEPS FORWARD TO OPEN IT. WOOLCOT CONTINUES FINGERING THROUGH THE MAIL. HE HEARS MARTHA BUT HIS ATTENTION IS SUDDENLY DIVERTED BY ONE OF THE ENVELOPES)

WOOLCOT:

(ALARMED) (TO ESTHER) A letter… from Miss Burton's Academy!

BUNTY:

(BEGGING SOFTLY) Please Martha? Don't tell him.

(LIFTS HIS VOICE) It isn't my fault! Blame the
OTHERS!

ESTHER:

Others? WHAT OTHERS?

WOOLCOT:

(TURNING TO BUNTY) Don't tell him what!

(MARTHA IS AT THE FRONT DOOR. SHE OPENS IT
SLOWLY, HER HEAD HANGING DOWN AS THE
ALWAYS CREAKING DOOR GRINDS OPEN.
GRADUALLY RAISING HER HEAD TO SEE WHO'S
ON THE OTHER SIDE, SHE RECEIVES A SHOCK,
GIVES A GASP, THEN STANDS BACK, MOUTH
WIDE OPEN AS SHE IS CONFRONTED BY TWO
POLICEMEN, THEIR BACKS TO THE AUDIENCE
HAVING ASCENDED THE STAIRS RISING FROM
THE ORCHESTRA PIT)

(WOOLCOT TURNS QUICKLY ABOUT, SEES THE
TWO POLICEMEN AT THE DOOR AND GOES WEAK
AT THE KNEES)

WOOLCOT:

Aaah … (RECOVERING HIS COMPOSURE) Oh, my
God!

(IN AN ATTEMPT TO GRASP THE SITUATION HE
ALTERS HIS DEMEANOUR TO ONE OF RELAXED
PLEASANTRY WHILE ESTHER EXCUSES MARTHA,
TAKING CHARGE AND APPROACHING THE
POLICEMEN)

(THE SERGEANT GREETS ESTHER FORMALLY. HE
DOFFS HIS HELMET)

SERGEANT:
Good morning, Mrs Woolcot … Captain......

ESTHER:
Good morning, Sergeant, Constable.

WOOLCOT:
(STEPPING FORWARD FROM BEHIND) (IN THE
ULTIMATE UNDERSTATEMENT) A lovely day, don't
you think… er, Sergeant?

SERGEANT:
(IGNORING HIS PLEASANTRY) We have received
advice from our station at Mount Victoria that a certain
Miss Judith Woolcot seems to have taken upon herself
unauthorized leave ….

(ESTHER LOOKS AS IF SHE IS ABOUT TO PASS
OUT. WOOLCOT STEADIES HER)

CONSTABLE:
(NOTING ESTHER'S CONDITION) (IN OCKER
LANGUAGE) …she's run away, Ma'am …. (TURNING
APOLOGETICALLY TO HIS SENIOR) Sorry, Sarge…

CONSTABLE:
(CONTINUING TO ADDRESS THE WOOLCOTS)
…from Miss Burton's Academy two days ago, Ma'am.

SERGEANT:
We've come to ask you Madam... Sir... have you had any
word from her at all?

MARTHA:

(STEPPING FORWARD) (TO THE POLICE) Your
honours … (TO ESTHER) Madam … (TO WOOLCOT)
Sir…., I think Bunty has something to tell you.

(BUNTY OPENS HIS MOUTH WHICH MOVES BUT
FROM WHICH NOTHING COMES)

SERGEANT:

Come on, young man. What's your news?

BUNTY:

(SPLUTTERS AND SUDDENLY SPITS IT OUT)
JUDY'S HOME!

WOOLCOT:

Whaaa … (TOO MUCH FOR HIM)

ESTHER:

(LOST FOR WORDS SHE MANAGES TO ASK)
Where, Bunty?

BUNTY:

In the barn.

ESTHER:

(IN SHOCK) I… I…(RECOVERING HER
COMPOSURE) (TO THE POLICE) Gentlemen, I think
you had better come with us…

(BLACKOUT)

(END OF SCENE)

END OF ACT ONE

ACT TWO

ACT TWO   SCENE ONE

'MISRULE' INTERIOR - EVENING

AT RISE:

> LIGHTS FADE UP. THE CHILDREN MINUS
> GENERAL MOPE ABOUT OUTSIDE A CLOSED
> DOOR ON ONE SIDE OF THE DRESS-CIRCLE
> WALK-WAY ON THE NURSERY. MEG IS
> CONSOLING THE YOUNGER ONES.

NELL:
Will she die? I think I will die with her, if she dies.

BUNTY:
Will she go to heaven, Meg? She will go to heaven, won't she?

MEG:
I don't know. Dr Gormiston said it was pneumonia…and she has a collapsed lung…

BABY:
Vhat's 'nu-moan-ya?

PIP:
(STILL IN HIS GRAMMAR SCHOOL UNIFORM) I think it's a chest problem…and Joods always had a weak chest…

NELL:
So she'll die!

(NELL BURSTS INTO TEARS FOLLOWED BY BABY)

(MARTHA EXITS JUDY'S ROOM, CLOSING THE
DOOR QUICKLY BEHIND HER. THE CHILDREN
SWOOP ON HER)

PIP:

How is she, Martha?

BUNTY:

Is she nearly dead?

NELL:

Will she go to heaven?

(ON SEEING THE CHILDREN MARTHA QUICKLY
USHERS THEM OFF TO BED)

MARTHA:

To bed now. Nell, and Baby, you are in Meg's room now.
(MEG WINCES) (TO THEM ALL) Come on. Time for
bed. I'll lead prayers. All right?

(THEY NOD YES)

PIP:

I'll finish my homework. (HE EXITS TO THE END OF
THE OFF PROMPT WALK-WAY)

BABY:

(TO JUDY'S DOOR) Gooth night, Judy.

(THEY EXIT INTO THE DOOR NEXT TO JUDY,
MARTHA BEHIND THEM)

(AT THE FOOT OF THE STAIRS WOOLCOT PACES.
ESTHER AND DR GORMISTON EXIT THE FIRST

FLOOR BEDROOM. MEG HANGS ABOUT AS THEY DESCEND THE STAIRS, ALAN FOLLOWING RESPECFULLY BEHIND. AT THE APPROPRIATE MOMENT MEG CAUTIOSLY FOLLOWS THEM DOWN, TRYING TO REMAIN UNNOTICED, EXCEPT TO ALAN)

(WOOLCOT ANXIOUSLY TAKES ESTHER IN HIS ARMS AND HOLDS HER TIGHTLY)

WOOLCOT:
Oh, please, God…PLEASE God?

ESTHER:
(UNCONVINCINGLY) It's not your fault…

(DR GORMISTON APPROACHES WOOLCOT, FOLLOWED BY ALAN. THERE IS A FORMALITY IN THEIR WALK TOWARDS THE WOOLCOTS. THEY ARE VERY SUBDUED AND SERIOUS. WOOLCOT IS DESPERATE)

GORMISTON:
(TAKING HIS TIME AND FORMALLY INTRODUCING ALAN) You know young Alan, here. In his final year.... medicine.... Sydney University.

ESHER/WOOLCOT:
Yes, yes. Of course.

ALAN:
Good evening, Mrs Woolcot...... (SHAKING HANDS) Sir…

WOOLCOT:

(HARDLY NOTICING) How is she, Doctor? Will she be all right?

GORMISTON:

(USHERING THEM AWAY FROM THE DOOR) I'm not sure. She's a fighter. I'll tell you that. She's certainly a fighter....

ESTHER:

But will she recover?

GORMISTON:

Weeell...we must be very careful. The next week or so will tell us.

WOOLCOT:

What do you mean?

GORMISTON:

The fever is subsiding. The pneumonia may be.... I say, may be showing signs of improvement. Another cold night in the bush... and she might well not be with us now. How head strong she must be.

WOOLCOT:

(NOW BESIDE HIMSELF) But will she be all right, man?

GORMISTON:

(ANNOYED) Captain Woolcot! This is a matter NOT entirely within my control! (SETTLING DOWN) I will give you my considered prognosis in one week. You must give her proper care... keep her warm, no boisterous activity... just peace and quiet. I have been through the medicines with Esther and Martha. Timing and rest are everything from now on.

ESTHER:
We won't let her down, Doctor.

WOOLCOT:
We certainly won't let her down. Rest assured in THAT.

(GORMISTON LOOKS APPREHENSIVELY AT THE DISTRESSED WOOLCOT)

WOOLCOT:
We won't be sending her back to boarding school, Doctor.

(GORMISTON IS FLABBERGASTED AT THE VERY IDEA)

GORMISTON:
(EMPHATICALLY) I SHOULD THINK NOT! There must be NO suggestion of such a move. ABSOLUTELY NOT!

(SUDDENLY HE SMILES AND LOOKS AT THEM BOTH IN A CARING MANNER, TRYING TO RELIEVE THEIR ANXIETY)

GORMISTON:
Look… it's up to you.

WOOLCOT:
Yes, doctor.

ESTHER:
Yes, doctor.

GORMISTON:

I will give you my prognosis.... next.... Monday.

ESTHER:

I'll show you out, doctor.

WOOLCOT:

Good night, Doctor.

(THEY ALL SHAKE HANDS BIDDING EACH OTHER A QUIET GOODNIGHT. DR GORMISTON IS ESCORTED THROUGH THE FRONT DOOR AS ALAN AWKWARDLY TRIES TO CATCHMEG'S EYE ON THE WAY OUT. AS GORMISTON LEAVES, ALAN GESTURES 'GOODNIGHT' TO HIM, THEN LOOKS TO WOOLCOT AS IF TO ASK SOMETHING, BUT WHO IS BUSY SAYING GOODNIGHT TO GORMISTON. ESTHER SMILES AT THE YOUNG ONES, HER EXPRESSION WELCOMING ALAN TO HANG ABOUT WITH MEG WHO QUICKLY USHERS HIM AWAY AND INTO THE DINING ROOM]

(LIGHTS UP ON DINING ROOM)

MEG:

(TO ALAN) Will Judy be all right?

ALAN:

Her best chance is to do exactly as she's told......
(PUSHING HIM TOWARDS THE DOOR) Doctor thinks she should get away from the coast, as far away as possible.... (LOOKING NERVOUSLY TOWARDS WOOLCOT WHO IS NOW ENGAGED WITH ESTHER) Perhaps....

MEG:

(PUSHING HIM THROUGH THE DOOR) Hurry...

ALAN:

As I said, he recommends taking her away. Doctor recommends a complete change of climate...

MEG:

Grandma wants us to bring her to Yarrahappini… It's their massive station in the outback. Several thousand square miles. And we're all invited to spend the Christmas holidays there.

ALAN:

(DISAPPOINTED) Would you be going?

MEG:

(SURPRISED) Of course. It's on the edge of the never-never. Hundreds of miles away.... wide open spaces.... a nice old house with big verandahs, where Esther grew up. There'll be picnics.... and bush dances … And the homestead is right next to Krangi-Bahtoo......

ALAN:

(TRYING TO SOUND EXCITED) Sounds wonderful …

(A PAUSE AS SHE NOTICES HIS DISAPPOINTMENT)

MEG:

I couldn't tell you in front of the others.

ALAN:

Tell me what?

MEG:

(STUMBLING) Father gave me a grilling… last night.

ALAN:

Oh?

MEG:

He asked me if your intentions were entirely honourable.

ALAN:

(LAUGHING) … and what did you say?

MEG:

Oh, it's so embarrassing…. I said… that I was not sure why he felt he needed to ask.

ALAN:

Well done, you!

MEG:

Oh Alan, I feel so much like an adult, but I'm not allowed to be. What should I do?

ALAN:

Don't worry, old thing. Just be patient. (PAUSE) Is your father really as harsh… as I'm told?

MEG:

He is, as far as Judy is concerned.

(ANOTHER PAUSE)

ALAN:

Miss Woolcot… Meg…. what do you say…. (PAUSE)… to falling…

MEG:

… in love?

ALAN:

Well… at the very least…. falling in 'like'?

MEG:

I'd say...

ALAN:

Yes?

MEG:

I'd say...

ALAN:

Yes, yes? What would you say? (HE GRABS HER PASSIONATELY AND THEY KISS)

(LIGHTS FADE DOWN)

(END OF SCENE)

ACT TWO   SCENE TWO

WOOLCOT'S STUDY – ONE WEEK LATER - MORNING

(SIGN ON PROSCENIUM ARCH READS, 'NEXT MONDAY')

AT RISE:

AT HIS DESK, WOOLCOT WEARING READING
GLASSES SIFTS THROUGH PAPERS. HE LOOKS UP,
IMPATIENTLY.

WOOLCOT:
(CALLING) Martha? Tea.

MARTHA:
(O.S.) Coming, sir.

WOOLCOT:
At last.

(THIS IS A GRUMBLE TO HIMSELF, BUT MARTHA
ENTERS AT THIS MOMENT WITH A TEA TRAY,
AND HEARS IT)

MARTHA:
Tea, Captain, is not something that can be hurried. (AS
SHE CONTINUES, SHE DEMONSTRATES, AS IF TO
A CHILD) I've been making tea, sir for thirty years and in
all that time, I have yet to discover a faster method than
taking the tea-leaves and putting them in the pot,... thus...
then boiling the water, and then pouring said water over the
tea-leaves... thus... and, then, waiting.

(A PAUSE. WOOLCOT FINALLY LOOKS UP)

You have to wait, sir, because if you don't wait, you don't
get no tea. It's the waiting that converts clear water into
coloured water, which is called tea. I don't know how they
do it in the army, sir, but that's how we do it in real life!

WOOLCOT:
Martha, why are you speaking to me as if I were a fool?

MARTHA:

I'm not going to answer that, sir, for fear of losing my job... I merely wanted to point out that tea has to be made. It does not appear by divine interruption. If you want miracles, sir, you're gonna have to pay me more.

WOOLCOT:

Thank you, Martha. That will be all.

MARTHA:

Of course, if you wish to experiment with the more exotic teas, you may have to wait a little longer…

WOOLCOT:

That will be ALL, Martha. Thank you very much!

(MARTHA EXITS AND WOOLCOT RETURNS TO HIS WORK. ESTHER ENTERS AND FOR A MOMENT, WHILE HE IS UNAWARE OF HER, SHE IS ABLE TO STUDY HIM.

HE IS TIRED. HE PUTS HIS HEAD ON THE DESK, AND CLOSES HIS EYES.

ESTHER MOVES BACK TO THE DOOR, MAKES A NOISE TO ANNOUNCE HER ARRIVAL. BY THE TIME SHE RE-ENTERS, WOOLCOT IS SITTING UP, ALERT)

WOOLCOT:

Has the doctor been?

ESTHER:

He's with her now. Said he's very encouraged. If she can

improve so much in such a short time, she must be incredibly strong.

WOOLCOT:

Or stubborn.

ESTHER:

He thinks we should get her away from the coast, as far as possible. And soon.

WOOLCOT:

That's easier said than paid for. If it means you and the family going with her.

ESTHER:

And you … ?

WOOLCOT:

Haah. Impossible.

(SHE COMES AND LOOKS AT THE DESK)

ESTHER:

You never used to bring work home. Is it important?

WOOLCOT:

Important? Tremendously! My signature in triplicate.... for six dozen shirts, six dozen vests, one gross of brass buttons, six dozen pairs of socks, knee length. Socks! I'm not a soldier any longer; I'm a haberdasher.

(ESTHER TAKES A LETTER FROM HER POCKET)

ESTHER:

About Judy... there's no problem. It's all arranged.

WOOLCOT:

How?

ESTHER:

Mother wants us to bring her to Yarrahappini ... as soon as possible.

WOOLCOT:

Does she?

ESTHER:

And to bring the little General, of course... because my parents have never set eyes on him. In fact, we're all invited. Martha as well. We're to spend the Christmas holidays there. You, too.

WOOLCOT:

(RATHER FORMAL) Very hospitable of them.

ESTHER:

Then you'll come? Father particularly asks that you accompany us. He says there's good shooting, and he has a new half-Arab colt for you to ride. And they've organised a special bush dance, just for us....

WOOLCOT:

And what happens if the Russians organise a landing on our beaches, while I'm cantering around the Never-Never. Who'll hand out the socks?

(ESTHER'S ENTHUSIASM IS DASHED. A PAUSE)

ESTHER:

You mean, you won't come?

WOOLCOT:

I can't.

ESTHER:

How long is it since you had a holiday?

WOOLCOT:

I don't need one. Life is one long holiday.... with the regiment.... and seven children.... and you.

ESTHER:

(UPSET) Thank you.

WOOLCOT:

I... didn't mean that quite the way it sounded.

ESTHER:

(PUTS THE LETTER ON HIS DESK) Read the letter for yourself.... when you have time. I'll take Judy and the other children, as soon as possible. If you choose not to accompany us, I'm sorry.

WOOLCOT:

I have no leave due.

ESTHER:

I looked up regulations. Military personnel may apply for compassionate leave, at any time.

WOOLCOT:

What? Run cap in hand to Colonel Bryant, at every domestic crisis?

ESTHER:

This is your daughter we're talking about. The one who nearly died.

WOOLCOT:

Please understand. I cannot come.

ESTHER:

Why? Would you demean yourself, to your fellow officers, running after your young wife?

(A PAUSE. HE DOES NOT ANSWER, BUT WE SUSPECT THERE MAY BE SOME TRUTH IN IT)

ESTHER:

Why did you marry me?

(SILENCE)

ESTHER:

More to the point, why did I marry you?

(MORE SILENCE)

ESTHER:

I know why. You were such a catch, that's why. And what was I? A simple country girl.... the poor, deprived daughter of a grazier with only a few thousand square miles of good sheep country to his name. And you, a widower.... a mature widower, with six children. Such a good catch. And now here we all are, living happily ever after, on an army captain's pay.

(LONG SILENCE. MARTHA ENTERS)

147

MARTHA:

Shall I take the tea, sir?

WOOLCOT:

(ANNOYED) I haven't had the tea yet.

MARTHA:

Beg your pardon.

(SHE EXITS)

ESTHER:

It'll get cold.

WOOLCOT:

I like it cold.

(WOOLCOT POURS SOME AND DRINKS IT, TRIES NOT TO GRIMACE)

ESTHER:

Cold?

WOOLCOT:

…Not very.

(HE OFFERS THE CUP TO ESTHER. SHE TAKES IT AND HAS A SIP)

ESTHER:

(SMILES) Drinking from the same cup. We haven't done this for years. It's almost indecent.

(SHE HANDS THE CUP BACK TO WOOLCOT, WHO
FROWNS AT HER, AS IF UNABLE TO KEEP UP
WITH THE MERCURIAL CHANGES IN MOOD)

ESTHER:

Don't frown like that, you old bear. It spoils your good
looks.

WOOLCOT:

Good looks…

ESTHER:

Well, I didn't marry you for your money.

WOOLCOT:

Hardly.

ESTHER:

Or your prospects of becoming Field Marshall Woolcot.

WOOLCOT:

Then why?

ESTHER;

(SMILES) Perhaps I was carried away by what you said.
That exciting, romantic proposal. I can hear it now.
(MIMICS, DOUR) "Miss Hassal, if you do not marry me, I
shall be very disappointed".

WOOLCOT:

(SMILES) You remember that?

ESTHER:

I remember everything. Every single thing. The regimental
ball and the officers in their dress uniforms, like painted

toy soldiers. My friends all jealous. Even Colonel Bryant acted as if he actually liked us... only briefly of course. How we danced.... and kept dancing.... and life was going to be full of magical colours, and never mind the grey days, because we cared for each other so much. I remember that....

(MARTHA RE-ENTERS SUDDENLY AND SMILING)

MARTHA:
The Doctor has just left. Says the worst is over. (EXCITEDLY) She's going to be all right! That's his prognosis. She's going to get better!

(WOOLCOT IS ANXIOUS. HE RUSHES TOWARDS HER WITH EMOTION)

MARTHA:
Oooh, Sir ... (REACTING)

WOOLCOT:
Where is he?

MARTHA:
Doctor couldn't wait. Three urgent visits before nightfall.

WOOLCOT:
(REGAINING HIS COMPOSURE) Of course. (HE SMILES AT ESTHER) Of course.

(BLACKOUT)

(END OF SCENE)

ACT TWO   **SCENE THREE**

DARKNESS – THE NIGHT-RIDER

AT RISE:

(SFX OF A FURIOUSLY FAST GALLOPING HORSE & RIDER)

WOOLCOT:
(O.S.) (OVER THE SFX) Come on. Come on!

(SFX AS THE EXHAUSTED HORSE AND RIDER REACH THEIR DESTINATION. INSIDE THE DARKNESS A LARGE OAK DOOR IS LIT AS IT DROPS DOWN FROM GRID (PART OF THE EXECUTIVE OF THE OFFICER'S QUARTERS AT VICTORIA BARRACKS). ON IT A BIG BRASS PLATE READS, 'COLONEL J. R. PHILIP BRYANT – COMMANDING OFFICER'. A DISHEVILLED WOOLCOT STAGGERS TOWARD THE DOOR, HIS BACK TO THE AUDIENCE. READYING, STRAIGHTENING HIMSELF, TAPS PROUDLY ON THE DOOR. SILENCE. HE TAPS MORE LOUDLY)

BRYANT:
(BELLOWS FROM BEHIND THE DOOR] (O.S.) Come. (WOOLCOT OPENS THE DOOR, ENTERS, CLOSING IT BEHIND HIM. CLICK)

WOOLCOT:
(O.S.) … Sir!

BRYANT:
Good evening, Captain Woolcot.

(WOOLCOT PRESSES ON IN HIS EXCITEMENT)

WOOLCOT:
The very best news.... Sir! She's going to be all right! The worst is over.

(SILENCE)

BRYANT:
(COLDLY) I'm pleased for you. (PAUSE) My time piece tells me (RAISING HIS VOICE) that you're late, Woolcot! Roll call was at TWENTY HUNDRED HOURS!

WOOLCOT:
But, sir?

BRYANT:
(EXAGGERATING HIS 'T's') No buts about it, Captain Woolcot!

WOOLCOT:
Yes, sir.

BRYANT:
DISMISSED!

WOOLCOT:
Yes, sir.

(THE DOOR OPENS SHARPLY - A HURT AND DEJECTED WOOLCOT EXITS SLOWLY, GENTLY CLOSING IT. HE TURNS SLOWLY TO LEAVE, THEN PAUSES. STARTING TO LEAVE A SECOND TIME HE AGAIN PAUSES, WAVES HIS HAND AS IF TO DISMISS THE IDEA. HE PAUSES ONCE MORE,

LOOKS TO THE DOOR, THEN BACK TOWARDS THE
AUDIENCE. HE RESOLVES TO GO AHEAD)

WOOLCOT:

(SHOUTS LOUDLY AND PROUDLY AT THE
CLOSED DOOR, HEAVILY EXAGGERATING THE
'P's' AND 'T') POMPOUS PRATT!!

(MUMBLING TO HIMSELF AS HE LEAVES) There.
(RESIGNED) I've blown it now!

ACT TWO   SCENE FOUR

WOOLCOT'S STUDY - EVENING

(THE CHILDREN WITH JUDY, RUGGED UP, ARE
FORMED IN A SEMICIRCLE ON THE FLOOR,
ESTHER AT THE HEAD)

AT RISE:

(THE MOOD IS HAPPY. THERE IS EXCITEMENT IN
THE ROOM.)

PIP:

Is it true? Are we going to Yarrahappini?

ESTHER:

Yes, we are. It's all arranged. We're leaving as soon as we
have clearance from Dr Gormiston.

JUDY:

(VOICE WEAK) And the billabong?

ESTHER:

Krangi-Bahtoo. Yes. And swimming.

BUNTY:

You'll have to get sick more often, Joods.

MEG:

Do we have to go?

PIP:

Haa! I knew it.

ESTHER:

Don't you want to go?

MEG:

(EMBARRASSED) Shhh ...

PIP:

Esther, is Father coming?

ESTHER:

(UPSET) No, I'm afraid not. He can't spare the time.

(ESTHER, UNHAPPY, EXITS SUDDENLY)

MEG:

Dopey!

BUNTY:

Stupid!

PIP:

What did I say?

(O.S. COMES THE SOUND OF A WEARY HORSE RETURNING, ITS RIDER DISMOUNTING)

(UNSEEN BY THE CHILDREN, A DISHEVILLED AND DEJECTED WOOLCOT APPEARS AT THE STUDY DOOR. THE CHILDREN REACT WITH USUAL CAUTION IN THEIR FATHER'S PRESENCE ON HEARING AND THEN SEEING HIM. THEY ALL STAND. ON HIM SEEING THEM, HE LIGHTS UP, HIS DEMEANOUR CHANGES AS HE GREETS THEM WARMLY)

CHILDREN:

(ALL) Good evening, father.

WOOLCOT:

Good evening to you all. And.... to the patient. (HE STRIDES OVER TO JUDY AND GIVES HER A KISS ON THE CHEEK) Are the others looking after you?

JUDY:

Oh, yes, Father. Everyone is being very kind.

(AS WOOLCOT TURNS, SMILING AT THE OTHERS, JUDY SCREWS UP HER FACE, RUNNING HER FINGER AROUND HER EAR IN A GESTURE SUGGESTING HER FATHER MAY HAVE LOST HIS MARBLES)

MEG:

Are you quite well, Father?

WOOLCOT:

I'm quite well. In fact … (PUFFING OUT HIS CHEST PROUDLY) I'm EXTREMELY well. And I've not enjoyed a day more in my life! (SMILES WITH ENORMOUS SATISFACTION, THEN YAWNS) Please excuse me. I'm suddenly quite tired. Would you mind very much if I say, goodnight?

(WITH WHICH, BEFORE ANY ANSWER, HE METHODICALLY GOES ROUND AND KISSES EACH OF THE YOUNGER CHILDREN, KISSES AND HUGS JUDY WHO IS STILL A LITTLE AWKWARD, SHAKES HANDS WITH PIP AND IS NOT SURE WHAT TO DO WITH MEG. SHE SAVES HIM FROM HIS EMBARRASSMENT, RUSHING TO HIM AND GIVING HIM A WARM HUG AS ESTHER RE-ENTERS)

ESTHER:

What's going on? Judy should be in bed. She's still under Doctor's strict orders. You all should be in bed. You little ones have been up far too long...

(ESTHER IS STARTLED, SUDDENLY SEEING WOOLCOT. SHE KNOWS SOMETHING IS DIFFERENT, BUT CANNOT BE SURE, WHAT IT IS)

ESTHER:

(SURPRISED) John... I didn't realise that you were back. Such a short trip.

WOOLCOT:

It was indeed ... wasn't it?

(HE LOOKS AT HER. THERE IS A PAUSE AS HER PERPLEXED DEMEANOUR ALTERS UNDER THE POWER OF A NEW LOVING SMILE. THEIR EYES LOCK TOGETHER AND HE SLOWLY APPROACHES

HER, TAKING HER GENTLY IN HIS ARMS AND
GIVING HER A VERY LONG, WARM HUG)

BUNTY:
Gee. That was a very long hug.

ESTHER:
It was rather.... wasn't it?

NELL:
I'll bet he's never done that before.

WOOLCOT:
You'd lose your bet. (AS HE TAKES HIS WIFE IN HIS
ARMS AGAIN)

PIP:
(WHISPERS) Bet… ter late than never.

MEG:
Shh. Be quiet, all of you...

(CHILDREN ALL FREEZE AS THERE IS A MOMENT
BETWEEN WOOLCOT AND ESTHER AWAY FROM
THE CHILDREN)

ESTHER:
John, is everything all right?

WOOLCOT:
It certainly is.

ESTHER:
Then.... (HER SPIRITS LIFTED) you'll come with us to
Yarrahappini ?

WOOLCOT:

(DRAWING BACK FROM AN EXCITED ESTHER)
Well... well.... that's a very interesting question. (PAUSE)

ESTHER:

It is. Indeed. That's why I asked it. (AN AWKWARD
PAUSE) (VERY PERPLEXED STILL) And what might
be the answer, dare I ask?

WOOLCOT:

(WITH A FROWN) ... I'm not really sure.

ESTHER:

... Not really sure?

WOOLCOT:

(CONFIDENT AT LAST) Well...

ESTHER:

You've said that.

WOOLCOT:

I have, haven't I.

ESTHER:

(BECOMING IMPATIENT) Yes.

WOOLCOT:

Well, (SMILES).... I think I must await the outcome.... of a
certain matter.

ESTHER:

What matter, if one may ask that also?

WOOLCOT:

One certainly may. It's just that… well, I may be (SPEAKS QUICKLY) court-marshalled for insubordination in respect of my commanding officer.

ESTHER:

What on earth....

WOOLCOT:

I think Colonel Bryant may have the impression.... that I called him....

ESTHER:

What might he think you called him?

WOOLCOT:

Well....

ESTHER:

Not again? (PAUSE) Well, what?

WOOLCOT:

I did in fact call him… (HIGHLIGHTING THE 'P's and 'T') a pompous pratt.

ESTHER:

Whaaat… (COVERS HER OPEN MOUTH) You said that!

CHILDREN:

(THE CHILDREN SNAP BACK TO LIFE. ALL GASP, MOUTHS WIDE OPEN. PIP FALLS OFF THE SIDE OF THE LOUNGE ON WHICH HE HAS BEEN RESTING INDELICATELY)

PIP:

(GENUINELY EMBARRASSED) Sorry...

WOOLCOT:

(EMBARRASSED BUT PROUD) Well... yes, I did... actually.

ESTHER:

(HUGGING HIM – SO PROUD) Oh, John.

(FINALLY WOOLCOT KISSES ESTHER GOODNIGHT, RETURNING, SMILING TO THE CHILDREN AS HE LEAVES THE ROOM WAVING HIS ARMS AND ROCKING HIS SHOULDERS ABOUT LIKE A HAPPY DRUNK)

PIP:

Wow!

BUNTY:

Gee, whiz.

JUDY:

Did Doctor G put father on some sort of medication?

ESTHER:

Come on, it really is time for bed. We've a long train trip to prepare for.

(LIGHTS FADE)

(END OF SCENE)

ACT TWO   SCENE FIVE

WOOLCOT'S STUDY - DAY

THE PROSCENIUM ARCH SIGN READS, 'ANOTHER
WEEK LATER'

AT RISE:

(A COUCH FOR THE CONVALESCING JUDY HAS
BEEN SET UP WHERE IT CAN CATCH THE SUN. A
TABLE WITH INVALID'S BRIC-A-BRAC IS NEXT TO
IT. MARTHA IS CLEANING. SUN STREAMS IN.

MEG ENTERS WITH A LARGE BUNCH OF
FLOWERS AND PUTS THEM IN A VASE NEXT TO
JUDY'S COUCH.

THE CHILDREN ARE PLAYING NOISILY AND
EXCITEDLY NEARBY)

MARTHA:
(TO MEG) It's good of the Captain to allocate his study to
Judy's convalescence.

MEG:
This was always the best room in the house.

(NOW JUDY GALLOPS INTO THE ROOM RIDING A
HOBBY HORSE. SHE IS BEING CHASED BY BUNTY,
NELL, BABY AND LITTLE GENERAL, ALL
DRESSED IN HOME-MADE RED INDIAN OUTFITS
AND WAVING CARDBOARD TOMAHAWKS AND
SPEARS)

BUNTY/BABY/ NELL:

(TOGETHER) Judy!

(THEY ALL ULULATE AND MAKE RED INDIAN
WAR WHOOPS AS THEY CHASE JUDY AROUND
THE ROOM.

PIP ENTERS. HE AND MEG WATCH IN
AMUSEMENT, AS JUDY ALLOWS HERSELF TO BE
CAUGHT, AND DRAGGED TO THE FLOOR AMID
THE WAR WHOOPS AND CHILDISH EXCITEMENT)

MARTHA:

(LOOKS OFF AND SEES SOMETHING) Children?
(NOBODY HEARS HER – SHOUTS) You kids…
QUIET.

(AS THEY QUIETEN)

MARTHA:

(POINTS OFF) Medicine man come to the house of big
warrior chief.

(MARTHA EXITS)

PIP:

Cripes.... Judy.... it's the quack!

(JUDY LEAPS ONTO THE COUCH, PULLS A RUG UP
TO HER NECK, CLOSES HER EYES AND PRETENDS
TO BE ASLEEP IN A LANGUID, VICTORIAN POSE.
SHE IS STILL WEARING HER INDIAN HEADBAND
WITH A FEATHER.

162

THE OLDER CHILDREN REACT, AS WOOLCOT AND
ESTHER APPEAR, WITH ALAN. HE CARRIES A
MEDICAL BAG)

BUNTY:

That's not a quack. That's Alan.

(MEG REACTS AT SEEING HIM. PIP MAKES A
LOVELORN FACE TO THE OTHER CHILDREN, WHO
EXPLODE IN SMALL GIGGLES)

WOOLCOT:

Be quiet, children. You all know Alan Courtney… Dr
Gormiston has asked him to visit us.

ALAN:

(SLIGHTLY SELF-CONSCIOUS) Meg…

MEG:

(SLIGHTLY SELF-CONSCIOUS) Alan…

NELL:

Are you a doctor now?

ALAN:

Not yet. But there's a measles epidemic.

PIP:

I'll bet that's kept Doctor Gormiston busy.

ALAN:

No.... he's in bed, with the measles. So, he's asked me to
give a progress report on Judy.

(THEY ALL WATCH AS ALAN SITS ON A CHAIR
BESIDE JUDY'S COUCH. HE LEANS CLOSE TO HER.

THE FEATHER IN HER HEADBAND TICKLES HIS
NOSE, AND HE SNEEZES.

THE YOUNGER CHILDREN LAUGH)

ESTHER:
Children… please…

(THIS IS A BAD START FOR ALAN, MADE RATHER
NERVOUS BY THE AUDIENCE ALL INTENTLY
WATCHING HIM.

HE REMOVES THE HEADBAND FROM JUDY. SHE
OPENS HER EYES)

JUDY:
(WEAK VOICE) Bless you, doctor…. ohhh… have I been
unconscious that many years? Alan…. have you graduated?

MEG:
Judy… stop it…

ALAN:
How are you feeling, Judy?

JUDY:
Exhausted… but a little better… thank you for asking.

(ALAN TRIES TO BEHAVE LIKE A DOCTOR, AS HE
TAKES HER WRIST AND CHECKS HER PULSE.

HE FROWNS.

164

HE TAKES A STETHOSCOPE FROM HIS BAG, AND
LISTEN TO JUDY'S HEART)

ALAN:
Good heavens!

ESTHER:
What is it?

ALAN:
Her heart's racing.

JUDY:
(IRISH BROGUE) 'Tis the thought of another train
journey... seein' how the last one was associated with such
calamity.

ESTHER:
(WARNINGLY) Judy …

WOOLCOT:
If you ask me, she's been tearing 'round the house again.

JUDY:
(IRISH BROGUE) Guilty, father... 'tis a perceptive one
you are, to be shure …

WOOLCOT:
(IGNORING HER NONSENSE) Alan, do you think you
can recommend to Dr Gormiston she be allowed to travel?

ALAN:
How far away is Yarrahappini?

ESTHER:

> Three hundred miles, by train. Then about twenty miles by wagon to the homestead.

ALAN:

> Well, it depends on you, Judy. That's a long trip... and you've had a serious illness. But you'd be better convalescing in the outback, where the air is hot.

JUDY:

> That's astonishing. I thought there was more hot air in Sydney, than the rest of Australia put together.

ESTHER:

> Judy... shoosh.

ALAN:

> (CHUCKLES) Will you promise to behave sensibly... both on the train and at Yarrahappini?

JUDY:

> Cross my heart and hope to die.

ALAN:

> Then I'll advise Dr Gormiston you're fit enough to go.
>
> (THE YOUNGER CHILDREN, WHO HAVE BEEN WAITING ANXIOUSLY, ALL CHEER. JUDY JUMPS OUT OF BED AS THEY ALL HUG HER.
>
> MEG HOVERS BY ALAN, AS HE PUTS AWAY THE STETHOSCOPE AND SHUTS HIS BAG)

ALAN:

> Meg... you'll enjoy the outback.

MEG:

Perhaps. But I'll miss Sydney.

(MEG AND ALAN JOIN ESTHER AND WOOLCOT. JUDY AND THE OTHERS MAKE PLANS IN THE BACKGROUND)

BUNTY:

Whatcha goin' to do now, Judy?

JUDY:

I'm going to convalesce in hot air.

NELL & BABY:

Tell us a story …

JUDY:

Uh-huh... stories are only for sitting around at night…

(SHE TAKES HER CERAMIC POT AND STARTS TO GO THROUGH IT, THE YOUNGER CHILDREN ALL EAGER AND ENTRANCED)

JUDY:

…what we want is something different... we want noises for journeys.

YOUNGER CHILDREN:

(TOGETHER) Noises! What noises? Journeys?

JUDY:

Just wait. (RIFLES THROUGH) What's here...? Stories for sitting... no? No… poems for special occasions…

(JUDY RIFLES THROUGH MORE PAPERS)

JUDY:

Let's see... poems for boring occasions… Ah, here it is, "Noises for Journeys"... "Journeys by Train!" This is it; Clickety-clack. (WHISPERS AND BUILDS) Clickety-clack, clickety-clack, (THE OTHERS JOIN) clickety-clack....

CHILDREN:

Clickety clack, clickety clack …

(SFX PICKS UP TRAIN NOISES THAT MERGE THE SCENES)

(LIGHTS GO DOWN GENTLY)

(END OF SCENE)

ACT TWO   SCENE SIX

YARRAHAPPINI RAILWAY STATION – SUNRISE

(SFX OF TRAIN NOISES LINK THE SCENES AND ACCOMPANY THE SLOWING TRAIN AS THE EARLY MORNING SUN RISES OVER THE PLATFORM. THE STAGE IS FILLS WITH STEAM AS THE LOCOMOTIVE AND ROLLING STOCK CREAK AND GROAN TO A STANDSTILL THENCE TO MERGE WITH THE FRESH SOUNDS OF BIRDS AND COUNTRY.

A SIGN ON THE PLATFORM READS 'YARRAHAPPINI'. BELOW IT – 'WELCOME TO THE OUTBACK'.

ON THE PLATFORM STAND MR & MRS HASSAL, MR GILLET AND TWO FARMHANDS TO HELP WITH LUGGAGE. THE CARRIAGE CONTAINING ESTHER AND THE CHILDREN IS REPRESENTED BY A MOVING EXTERIOR PANEL OR PROJECTION OF A MOVING TRAIN. THE WOOLCOT'S CARRIAGE APPROACHES TOWARDS PROMPT WITH THE CHILDREN CROWDED AT TWO WINDOWS LOOKING ABOUT THE PLATFORM)

AT RISE:

THE TRAIN COMES TO REST. THE DOOR IS OPENED EXTERNALLY BY A GUARD AND THE CHILDREN STUMBLE OUT, EACH CARRYING A BAG WHILE ESTHER, MEG AND PIP MAKE UP THE REAR STRUGGLING WITH SEVERAL LARGE SUITCASES)

BUNTY:

(SHOUTS) There they are. Over there! (AS HE POINTS HE NEARLY POKES NELL'S EYE OUT AND SHE QUICKLY MOVES OUT OF THE WAY)

NELL:

Look out, will you please, Bunty. That's my eye.

BUNTY:

Sorry, sis. (POINTING MORE CAREFULLY) There they are.

PIP:

They're both here. Grandpa and little grandma! Come on…. (HE RACES AHEAD OF THE OTHERS AS JUDY MOVES SLOWLY BEHIND WITH MEG)

BABY/BUNTY:
> Yeaaah! (THEY START RUNNING)

(THE GUARD AND FARMHANDS RETRIEVE THE
BAGGAGE, SUITCASES AND ALSO A LARGE
TRUNK. THE GUARD SALUTES ESTHER, THE TWO
FARMHANDS SHAKING HER HAND AND BOWING
MOST RESPECTFULLY AS SHE FOLLOWS THE
CHILDREN ONTO THE PLATFORM, THE HASSALS
HURRYING TOWARDS THEM)

(THE STEAM AND SFX OF THE PUFFING
LOCOMOTIVE CONTINUES AS THE WARMEST OF
GREETINGS TAKE PLACE BETWEEN ALL. MR
HASSAL, HIS NOW GAMMY LEG EVIDENT AND
MRS HASSAL, A TINY FUSSING WOMAN, OPEN
THEIR ARMS TO RECEIVE THEIR LOVED ONES AS
MR GILLET, A GAUNT AND REFINED OLDER
LOOKING MAN FROM THE OLD COUNTRY,
RESPLENDENT WITH A TRIMMED WHITE BEARD
STANDS BACK)

(MR GILLET SOON GRAVITATES SPECIFICALLY
TO JUDY AND MEG AS THE GREETINGS
CONTINUE. PIP RUSHES TO MR HASSAL WHO IS
WITH THE STATION MASTER SIGNING A RECEIPT
FOR A MAILBAG BEING PASSED BY THE GUARD
TO ONE OF THE FARMHANDS. THERE IS A LOUD
WHISTLE BLAST (SFX) AS A FINAL HUGE BLAST
OF STEAM SWAMPS THE STATION AND WE HEAR
THE TRAIN MOVING OFF AGAIN)

MR HASSAL:
> (TO PIP) What is it, my boy?

170

PIP:

(TO MR HASSAL) Will you teach me wool-classing? Remember, we started ... last time … Will you?

MR HASSAL:

Of course, Philip. You remembered that … ?

(THE SMOKE CLEARS AS THE RAILWAY STATION SIGN RISES AND THE PLATFORM TURNS INTO A LARGE DRAY/BUGGY WTH TWO LONG SHAFTS PROJECTING AT THE FRONT, POINTING TOWARDS OFF PROMPT, INTO THE WINGS. SFX SUGGESTS THERE ARE TWO HORSES ABOUT TO HAUL IT ALONG. THE LUGGAGE IS LOADED AND ALL CLIMB ABOARD AS WOODEN SIDES TO THE DRAY RISE INCLUDING AT FRONT, A LARGE BENCH [DRIVER'S SEAT] WITH BACKREST. THERE ARE FOUR PASSENGER BENCHES [2 x2 FACING EACH OTHER] SET BEHIND THE DRIVERS. THE HASSALS SIT BETWEEN THE CHILDREN, MRS HASSAL NEXT TO BABY, MR HASSAL NEXT TO ESTHER. THE TWO FARMHANDS CLIMB UP FRONT SITTING NEXT TO EACH OTHER, ONE TAKING THE REINS AND LOOKING BACK TO CHECK ALL ARE ABOARD)

FARMHAND:

(LOOKING BACK AND THEN DIRECTLY AT MR HASSAL) All set, boss?

MR HASSAL:

(CALLING BACK) Right to go, Mackie!

(THE LEAD FARMHAND CRACKS HIS WHIP)

FARMHAND:

(TO THE HORSES) C'mon me lov'lies. Time t' go.

(SFX OF THE DRAY ROLLING OFF AS THE
PROJECTION REVEALS THE MOVING
COUNTRYSIDE, AND SOON THE RAW OUTBACK,
AMID SOUNDS OF THE HEAVY DRAY
TRAVELLING A ROUGH COUNTRY ROAD. THE
AUDIENCE P. O. V. NOTES THE CONTRAST
BETWEEN THE CITY AND THE OUTBACK)

MR HASSAL:

(TO ESTHER) Oh, child…it's so good to see you….
(LOOKING TO THE CHILDREN) ….and the whole tribe.
And … (TO JUDY) I do believe this time it's thanks to
you, that we have you all with us … a second time.

BUNTY:

Yeah… run away from boarding school again, Joods!

ESTHER:

Oh, father... mother….

MR HASSAL:

(TICKLING GENERAL UNDER THE CHIN) Hello, little
one. I've not seen you before. Such a big fellow already.
It's an honour to meet you, sir. (HE SHAKES THE
GENERAL'S HAND)

NELL:

He's just getting fat, grandpa.

MR HASSAL:

Oh, how can you say that, Nellie. He's just growing up...
his way.

172

MRS HASSAL:

(TO JUDY) You must be exhausted after your journey.

JUDY:

Absolutely not, little Grandma. I'm so looking forward to riding 'Jackson'. Can he be mine while we're here?

MR HASSAL:

Are you up to riding... already?

MRS HASSAL:

We can decide all that later, can't we.

MR HASSAL:

(GESTURING TO MR GILLET) And… I'm sure you all remember Mister Gillet.

(MR GILLET ACKNOWLEDGES, LIFTING HIS HAT AT THE BACK)

MR GILLET:

(TO ALL) Welcome to the 'OUTBACK'!

(THE FILM SHOWS OFF THE DRY, BROWN PLAINS TO THE MOUNTAINS. THE SUN LIFTING A LITTLE HIGHER AND THEY ENTER THE GRAND GATES OF THE SPRAWLING HASSAL PROPERTY "YARRAHAPPINI STATION")

(MR GILLET PARTICULARLY NOTICES MEG AS HE SITS DIRECTLY BEHIND HER TALKING OVER HER SHOULDER. THE WAGON BOUNCES OVER SOME PARTICULARLY ROUGH BUMPS)

FARMHAND:

Look out behind. Bit of a rough patch ahead.

(THE DRAY SLEWS ABOUT AS IT NEGOTIATES THE BUMPS)

MR GILLET:

(CALLING TO THE HASSALS AND EYEING OFF MEG) My, they've grown since their last visit.

MRS HASSAL:

(INNOCENTLY) Yes, Mister Gillet... they grow up so quickly these days.

(MR GILLET CASTS AN EYE MEG'S WAY AT THIS)

PIP:

(LOOKING ABOUT HIM) Wow... this is how to travel. Beats the tram any old day. (TO MR HASSAL) Can I help with the cattle drafting again, grandpa?

(THE CHILDREN ASK THEIR QUESTIONS RAPID-FIRE)

JUDY:

Is Tettawonga still here, grandpa?

MEG:

What about the horses... can I have 'Bonny Prince Charlie', grandpa?

JUDY:

(QUICKLY PRESSING HER CLAIM) And pleeease ... can I have 'Jackson', grandpa? Please?

MRS HASSAL:

Hey… one at a time? Remember your grandpa's not hearing so well these days. And Judy… you must take things quietly for a little while…

NELL:

(TO MRS HASSAL) Bunty wants to know if you still make 'blackberry tart?

BUNTY:

(EXCITEDLY) Yes, that's exactly what I WAS wanting to know!

JUDY:

(LOOKING INTO THE DISTANCE) Ooooh… isn't that beautiful…

BABY:

I f'ink it boo'ful too.

MRS HASSAL:

(HER ARM AROUND BABY) Do you, Baby? Do you know something?

BABY:

Vh'at does I know, g'an ma?

MRS HASSAL:

I think it's so beautiful... that I never want to leave. (SQUEEZING HER)

MEG:

It's romantic…

MR GILLET:

(CALLING FROM BEHIND) It's the outback… and there's only one way they'll take me out from here.

MR HASSAL:

Mister Gillet's right. This is surely God's own country.

MRS HASSAL:

But sometimes it can be cruel. We treat it with respect.

(THE SUN HAS RISEN A LITTLE HIGHER AS INTO VIEW COME THE GATES OF "YARRAHAPPINI HOMESTEAD", ITS MAGNIFICENT HOMESTEAD IN THE DISTANCE)

MR HASSAL:

…nearly there…

MRS HASSAL:

I'll bet you're all hungry after such a long journey…

BUNTY:

I'll bet…

MRS HASSAL:

And you might receive a surprise, young Bunty.

BUNTY:

Oh boy! Blackberry tart!

(LIGHTS FADE)

(END OF SCENE)

ACT TWO   SCENE SEVEN

'YARRAHAPPINI STATION' - MORNING

(SIGN ON THE PROSCENIUM ARCH READS 'NEXT
MORNING')

(THE EARLY MORNING SUN SHINES ABOVE A
REAR PROJECTION DEPICTING SANDSTONE
BUILDINGS, COTTAGES, OUT HOUSES, THE
HOMESTEAD IN THE DISTANCE, THE WOOLSHED
WITH ITS TREES AND BILLABONG NEARBY,
PADDOCKS AND HOLDING PENS ETC. A LARGE
SIGNPOST STANDS PROMINENTLY, THREE
QUARTERS ACROSS STAGE FROM PROMPT
CORNER. SEVERAL ATTACHED SIGNS POINT
WITH ARROWS INDICATING DIRECTION AND
DISTANCE TO KEY FACILITIES ON THE
PROPERTY.
INCLUDED IS THE 'WOOLSHED' - 800 YARDS,
'STORE SHEDS' – 256 YARDS, 'WORKERS
COTTAGES' - 30 YARDS, 'HORSE CORRALS' –
EQUINE FLAT - 40 YARDS, 'AGRICULTURE FIELDS'
- 500 YARDS, 'MUSTERING YARDS' 950 YARDS,
'STOCK YARDS GENERAL' – 500 YARDS, 'CATTLE
PENS' – 300 YARDS. THE AUDIENCE'S
PERSPECTIVE IS OF DISTANCE AND A WELL
ESTABLISHED AND MASSIVE PROPERTY)

AT RISE:

ESTHER, JUDY, [HOLDING THE GENERAL'S HAND],
NELL, BABY AND MRS HASSAL ENTER FROM OFF
PROMPT AND PAUSE, ABOUT TO WALK TO THE
SIGNPOST)

MRS HASSAL:

(TO ESTHER) Are the boys coming? I wouldn't like them to miss out …

(THE QUIET IS BROKEN BY SUDDEN SHOUTING IN THE DISTANCE)

BUNTY:

(O.S.) Hurry up, Pip, or I'll knock the dunnee door down.

PIP:

(O.S.) Buzz off, urchin.

BUNTY:

(O.S.) Hurry, Pip. I'm BURSTING!!

JUDY:

Does that answer your question, little grandma?

ESTHER:

(TO HER MOTHER) Oh dear…. I'm sorry. That isn't usual.

(NELL AND BABY SNIGGER)

MRS HASSAL:

Don't be silly. I'm well used to the personal habits of young men out here.

(PIP RUNS ONTO THE STAGE DOING UP HIS FLY)

PIP:

Sorry I'm late, Li'll Grandma.

(MRS HASSAL SMILES AT HIM AS BUNTY RACES
IN A LITTLE AFTER HIM)

MRS HASSAL:
Well… Good morning, Bunty.

BUNTY:
(LOOKING EMBARRASSED) Golly, gee.
(REMEMBERING HIS MANNERS) Good morning,
Grandma.

ESTHER:
That's better, Bunty.

BUNTY:
I'm tired already, Grandma.

MRS HASSAL:
Well, don't be. There's quite a way to go.

(THEY SET OFF ON THEIR JOURNEY. FIRST STOP,
THE SIGNPOST)

MRS HASSAL:
(TO THE CHILDREN) Now wherever you go, remember
how to get back to here. (TOUCHES THE SIGNPOST)
To this sign. Ask any of the boys and they'll help you.

CHILDREN:
Yes, Grandma.

(AS MRS HASSAL SPEAKS, THE REAR PROJECTION
SLOWLY MOVES, REVEALING A BACKDROP THAT
OPENS NEAR THE FRONT OF THE LARGE AND
IMMACULATELY MAINTAINED HOMESTEAD

GARDEN. THE PARTY WALKS WITHOUT MOVING.
THE SOUND OF A DIDGERIDOO FADES UP AS
THEY PASS TETTAWONGA, THE BENT, OLD
ABORIGINAL SITTING OUTSIDE A BARK HUMPY
IN THE DISTANCE)

BUNTY:

I remember HIM… and his long music pipe.

MRS HASSAL:

Ah, yes, dear Tettawonga… not as young as he used to
be…

JUDY:

Besides his stories, he did something REALLY important,
didn't he?

BUNTY:

How do you know? Showoff?

MRS HASSAL:

Judy's quite right, Bunty. He saved your mother... and her
mother from bushrangers.

(JUDY MAKES A FACE AT BUNTY AS IF TO SAY
"TOLD YOU")

NELL:

Bushrangers? Real BUSHRANGERS?

MRS HASSAL:

REAL as you would EVER not want to see. For soon after
we first came here, Mister Hassal was cattle drafting, when
they attacked … and Tettawonga killed them both with his
tomahawk!

JUDY:

Urrrrgh! Imagine the blood?

BUNTY:

Golly! Real live bushrangers… here and everything!

BABY:

Is farva thafe at home… wivout hith thom-a-hawk?

PIP:

Bushrangers don't come up the Parramatta road anymore, Baby.

JUDY:

Just WITCHES, like her of the evil mind, Aldith.

BABY:

Ith Aldiff coming here too, grandma?

JUDY:

Over my dead body, Baby. Worry not!

MRS HASSAL:

Heavens, you two… she can't be THAT bad!

(TETTAWONGA GIVES A FRIENDLY WAVE AND THEY ALL WAVE BACK. THEY WALK ON AND ARRIVE AT A LARGE SHED CLEARLY MARKED 'STORES'. AT FRONT, THE DOOR IS BOLTED WITH A HEAVY PADLOCK WHICH ATTRACTS THE CHILDREN)

NELL:

Oh, let's go in. It looks like a treasure house in a book.

MRS HASSAL:

That building holds the STORES.

BUNTY:

Boy… food! Let's raid it …

PIP:

May we go in please, little grandma?

MRS HASSAL:

You must ask Mister Gillet. He keeps the keys. He'll be back shortly. He's taken Meg riding.

(JUDY IMMEDIATELY LOOKS CONCERNED)

MRS HASSAL:

(SHE POINTS TOWARD THE 'COTTAGES' IN THE PROJECTION) He lives over there. (POINTING MORE CLEARLY) See…over there… cottage near the water tank.

JUDY:

I didn't know Meg had gone riding, little grandma?

PIP:

Nor I?

MRS HASSAL:

It was one of those things… an accident I suppose. Mister Gillet just happened to be walking 'Bonnie Prince Charlie' past the homestead and Meg… well that was her horse, last time.

(THE PROJECTION REVEALS TWO TINY SANDSTONE OUTHOUSES FROM WHICH SEVERAL

WORKMAN WAVE TO THEM. THE CHILDREN RETURN THEIR WAVES AS THEY PASS. IMMEDIATELY NEXT DOOR IS A SQUATTER'S LEAN-TO. OUTSIDE STANDS A BATTERED OLD BROWN STOCKMAN SMOKING AN OLD CLAY PIPE)

MRS HASSAL:
Hello, Blue.

BLUE:
(RAISES HIS HAT TO HER) Mornin', M'ss H.

MRS HASSAL:
(TO CHILDREN) This is 'Blue'. He was here... even before us. He's one of the family.

MEG:
(CLOSEST TO HIM AND NOTICING THE SMELL) Wouldn't you like to live in one of the cottages? (SHE POINTS) Over there?

SQUATTER:
Not to mention.

PIP:
What do you do here?

SQUATTER:
Smoke.

PIP:
But on Sundays, and all through the evenings?

SQUATTER:

Smoke.

BABY:

On Cwismas Day. Zen what does you do?

SQUATTER:

Smoke.

JUDY:

How long have you been here?

SQUATTER:

Forget. An 'underred yee's … give or take....

JUDY:

Don't you ever forget how to talk?

(THE SQUATTER IS NOT ENJOYING THIS)

MR GILLET:

(HELPING THE SQUATTER) It's the squatter's wish that he stays right here forever.

(THE SQUATTER PULLS A BROWN HAT DOWN HARD ON HIS HEAD, TURNS AND GOES INSIDE THE LEAN-TO)

(UNHEARD BY THE AUDIENCE, THE LITTLE GROUP CHATS BUSILY. PROMINENT ON THE PROJECTION COMES ANOTHER LARGER STONE BUILDING IN THE DISTANCE THAT ZOOMS IN CLOSER NEAR PROMPT CORNER. IT IS MARKED 'SUPPLIES –OFFICE'. AT PROMPT CORNER NOW WALKS MEG AND BEHIND HER, MR GILLET,

HOLDING TWO SETS OF REINS BELONGING TO
TWO HORSES (UNSEEN), TYING THEM TO A
WOODEN 'T' BAR [ACCOMPANIED BY SFX] AS IF
BELONGING BEHIND ONE WALL OF THE
PROJECTED STONE BUILDING WHICH HAS
STOPPED MOVING AND IS FIXED. THE COUPLE
ARE UNSEEN AND INDEPENDANT OF MRS
HASSAL'S GROUP ELSEWHERE ON THE STAGE)

MR GILLET:

You remind me so much of my little sister who died.
Perhaps if she were alive now I mightn't be quite
so…contemptible?

(MEG BLUSHES AND CANNOT LOOK AT HIM)

MEG:

Please excuse me, Mister Gillet. I'm not entirely
comfortable with you telling me all this.

MR GILLET:

Don't take offence, Miss Meg. The last thing I wish is to
cause any awkwardness between us. (PAUSE) I think I
would like you to know that…if it's not too forward of me?

MEG:

(GATHERING HERSELF) I don't think you're
contemptible. Not in the least.

(THE RIBBON THAT TIES MEG'S HAIR HAS COME
LOOSE AND FALLS OFF. HER HAIR FALLS FREE
OVER HER SHOULDERS AS SHE GIVES A TINY
GASP AND IS EMBARRASSED. SHE REACHES
BEHIND HER HEAD, MR GILLET LOOKING TO HER.
HE PICKS UP THE PALE BLUE RIBBON AND

MOVES CLOSE TO HER AS IF TO RE-TIE IT. MEG
SEEMS TO BE ACCEPTING OF THE IDEA.)

MR GILLET:

(HOLDING UP THE RIBBON) May I keep it…as a
memory of your visit? I will treasure it always… if you
would agree?

MEG:

(EXCITED AND INNOCENT) If you would…oh, if you
would!

(THEY BECOME AWKWARD TOGETHER AS THE
CHILDREN WITH LITTLE GRANDMA APPROACH)

MRS HASSAL:

Good morning, Mr Gillet. Someone I know… has
something to ask you...

JUDY:

Begging your pardon, sir? We would like to borrow the
keys….to the store room? …if you have no objection…of
course?

(MEG IS EMBARRASSED AT THE POSSIBLE
CIRCUMSTANCES HER LOOSE HAIR MAY
SUGGEST)

MR GILLET:

Most happy to oblige, Miss Woolcot. They're back at the
cottage. I'll arrange it before the picnic.

MRS HASSAL:

(TO BUNTY) Can you wait until tomorrow, young Bunty?

186

BUNTY:

(DISAPPOINTED) Yes, grandma.

(DURING THIS EXCHANGE MR GILLET QUIETLY MUMBLES TO HIMSELF. JUDY LOOKS AT HIM STRANGELY)

MR GILLET:

(MUMBLING TO HIMSELF) "Oh that I was where I would be! Then I would be where I am not....

JUDY:

(REALISING SOMETHING) Is that poetry you're quoting to yourself, Mr Gillet?

MR GILLET:

I? Indeed no. What makes you think so, Miss Judy?

JUDY:

I can hear it distinctly. Your eyes are saying it, and your left ear, not to mention the ends of your moustache.

(HE SHUTS HIS EYES AND HOLDS HIS LEFT EAR, THEN COVERS HIS MOUSTACHE)

MR GILLET:

What can they be saying?
> "Oh that I was where I would be!
> Then I would be where I am not;
> But where I am I still must be,
> And where I would be I cannot".

JUDY:

Meg, I wish you would stop treading on my toes.

(MR GILLET, TAKING A SWIG FROM HIS HIP
FLASK STEPS OVER TO SPEAK TO MRS HASSEL AS
JUDY ANXIOUSLY CATCHES MEG'S EAR)

JUDY:

What is it with Mr Gillet?

MEG:

How very 'gallant' he is.

JUDY:

Oh Meg, you're such a pushover…besides he is older
than…father!

MEG:

Oh, don't be so silly…I didn't mean…

MRS HASSAL:

(TO THE CHILDREN) Mr Gillet was asking why Miss
Martha didn't come to Yarrahappini. I told him she is
looking after your father, who cannot come.

NELL:

Yes, li'l Grandma. She is.

BUNTY:

Poor Martha.

MRS HASSAL:

Now, that will be enough, young man. (TO THEM ALL)
Come on.

(MR GILLET GRAVITATES BACK TO MEG,
GESTURING TO HOLD BACK BEHIND THE OTHERS

AS THEY MOVE OFF THE STAGE AS IF
CONTINUING ON THEIR JOURNEY)

MR GILLET:

Miss Meg, would you please honour me with the pleasure
of your company again tomorrow? I'll replace the worn
shoe on Bonnie Prince Charlie's rear hoof. It's obviously
bothering him and you can try him out again. I'd be ever so
pleased if you would... and grateful?

MEG:

Well... yes ... I think that would be all right. Yes.
(SMILING AT HIM) I think I'd like that.

(JUDY HAS NOTICED MEG IS MISSING AGAIN AND
COMES BACK FOR HER)

JUDY:

(MR GILLET IS ANNOYED - JUDY IGNORES IT) Meg,
I was wondering where you were ...

(MR GILLET TAKES THE HINT, HAS ANOTHER
SWIG FROM HIS HIP FLASK AND TURNS TOWARD
THE HORSES WHICH ARE BECOMING NOISY) I'll
attend to the horses.

MEG:

(CALLING BACK) Give 'Bonnie Prince Charlie' a pat
from me.

MR GILLET:

I most certainly will. I'll see you in the morning, Miss Meg.

JUDY:

(ANNOYED AND PULLING HER AWAY) Come on!

(BLACKOUT)

(END OF SCENE)

ACT TWO   SCENE EIGHT

WOOLCOT'S STUDY - MORNING

AT RISE:

> LIGHTS GENTLY FADE UP ON MARTHA DUSTING
> FURNITURE AS WOOLCOT PERUSES THE BOOKS
> ON A SHELF. HE LIFTS A LOOSE SHEET OF PAPER.

WOOLCOT:
(TO MARTHA) Very quiet…

MARTHA:
(CONTINUING THE DUSTING) Yes, sir.

WOOLCOT:
(HALF READING – HALF REFLECTING) Quite
peaceful, in fact.

MARTHA:
Yes, sir. (THEN REMEMBERING) Oh, I quite
forgot…Mister Courtney called.

(HIS FACE LIGHTS UP)

WOOLCOT:
Mister Courtney, you say?

MARTHA:
Yes, sir.

(SHE TAKES AN ENVELOPE FROM HER POCKET
AND HANDS IT TO HIM)

MARTHA:
He asked me to give you this.

WOOLCOT:
Thank you, Martha.

WOOLCOT:
(OPENING IT AND READING) Fine young man. Going
to be a doctor, you know?

(READING ON)

WOOLCOT:
Er…Mister Courtney wishes to see me … ask my advice....

(MARTHA NODS, A KNOWING SMILE ON HER
FACE)

MARTHA:
Yes, sir. He's waiting outside.

WOOLCOT:
(TAKEN ABACK) What…here? … Now?

MARTHA:
Yes, sir.

WOOLCOT:

(WITH HIS NEW CONFIDENCE) Why didn't you tell me?

MARTHA:

You didn't ask …... sir.

WOOLCOT:

Well, I'm asking?

MARTHA:

What? (PAUSE) (WOOLCOT GLARES) What, are you asking... sir? (SHE STANDS WITHOUT MOVING)

WOOLCOT:

(RAISING HIS VOICE) Send him in, woman! Send him in.

MARTHA:

(ENJOYING HERSELF) Oh. (PRETENDING TO NOW UNDERSTAND) Yes, sir!

(WOOLCOT RETURNS TO READ FROM THE SHEET OF PAPER, THEN TO GREET ALAN FORMALLY AS HE ENTERS)

WOOLCOT:

I've only this minute received your note, my boy. Please sit down.
(THERE IS A STIFF FORMALITY AND NERVOUSNESS AS BETWEEN THE TWO MEN. THEY ARE BOTH INSECURE)

WOOLCOT:

You mentioned... something about advice.

ALAN:

Yes, sir. (EMBARRASSED, HE PAUSES, THEN ON THE SPUR OF THE MOMENT, CHANGES THE SUBJECT) I've just received a letter from Yarrahappini.

WOOLCOT:

Have you?

ALAN:

Yes, and it was suggested that you might appreciate a little company... with everyone away. A bit of cheering up.

WOOLCOT:

You're corresponding, you and Meg?

ALAN:

No, no. Well, yes. But this letter's from Judy. Her health is much improved... but of course, you'd know that from Mrs Woolcot's letters.

(WOOLCOT SHAKES HIS HEAD "NO")

WOOLCOT:

The only intelligence I've received, apart from one brief letter, is a clutch of postcards, with no information whatever!

ALAN:

Probably in a hurry … always on the go. But you do know all about that.

WOOLCOT:

Oh, yes. I know all about that.

(ALAN SMILES)

ALAN:

I quite understand, sir.

(WOOLCOT RAISES THE SHEET OF PAPER AND
READS)

WOOLCOT:

I was just reading this.... before you arrived. Listen.
(READS)
> "I think that little children, when they die,
> Return to where they came from in the sky
> And every child becomes a shining star,
> God doesn't care how good or bad they are.
> And in the evening when our Lord looks down,
> The stars are all the jewels in his crown."

ALAN:

Judy?

WOOLCOT:

Yes. (A PAUSE) Extraordinary girl. I doubt I'll ever
understand her ... but I do like that. (HE PLACES THE
POEM BACK GENTLY ON AN OCCASSIONAL
TABLE) (CHANGING THE SUBJECT) You
mentioned...

ALAN:

Yes, sir. Well, sir… you see, sir... actually... there have
been lots of letters. Every day.

WOOLCOT:

From Judy?

ALAN:

Oh no, sir. From Miss Woolcot... I mean, Meg. (A PAUSE) Could I ask your opinion in a fairly delicate matter?

WOOLCOT:

From Meg, eh. (THINKS DEEPLY) Well... of course. (REVERTS TO HIS NATURAL SENSE OF REASONING) All sound military strategies, before being taken, are based on open and frank discussion. So tell me, my boy... what is it? (MORE PERSONAL) My advice is not often sought ... not these days.

ALAN:

Well...I don't see it quite in terms of the military ... no disrespect, sir. But ... do you think it would be inappropriate for me to visit Yarrahappini Station during Miss Woolcot's time there?

WOOLCOT:

Heavens, boy? No need to ask me. It's Margaret who would need to invite you, and she in turn would need to have asked her...

ALAN:

(NERVOUSLY INTERRUPTING) She already has, sir.

WOOLCOT:

Has she? Has she indeed? (PAUSE) The Postmen of Australia have been busier than I thought. (PAUSE) I see. Ummm... And ... I could do with a bit of cheering up, eh?

ALAN:

It was Judy. She wrote words to that effect .... But she's not very respectful.

WOOLCOT:

She never has been ... Please, I'd like to hear it.

(WITH SOME TREPIDATION, ALAN TAKES A LETTER FROM HIS POCKET AND READS FROM IT. HE STANDS UP TO DO SO)

ALAN:

"Dear Stethescope ... (COUGHS)... My pulse is fine. Grandpa and Little Grandma are wonderful... which is a relief after...." (STOPS) Are you sure, sir?

WOOLCOT:

Please ...

ALAN:

(CONTINUES READING) "... a relief after my male parent, the Squire of 'Misrule', and his foibles..."

WOOLCOT:

Hmph.

ALAN:

(CONTINUES) "The sky is bluest blue, and everything smells as clean as fresh gum leaves. We ride horses, have picnics at Krangi-Bahtoo billabong, and there's to be bush dance on Friday in the woolshed. Esther says it's a pity father isn't here, because he's such a splendid dancer... which I find almost impossible to believe...."

(HE GIVES AN APOLOGETIC GLANCE AT
WOOLCOT)

WOOLCOT:
Do continue.

ALAN:
(READS ON) "How could those old bones of his actually
dance?"

WOOLCOT:
Heaven forbid. (PAUSE) Hmmmph. … old bones, eh?

ALAN:
Sorry, sir.

WOOLCOT:
Not your fault, my boy. Most illuminating. (REACHING
TOWARDS A DECANTER) Care for a port?

ALAN:
No, thank you. I should be getting home.

WOOLCOT:
Kind of you to "cheer me up". You know… I've been
thinking … yes … I've been thinking …

ALAN:
Have you, sir?

WOOLCOT:
Indeed I have, young man … (TO HIMSELF) Sometimes,
even court-marshals have to wait.

ALAN:

(LOOKING COMPLETELY BEWILDERED) They do, sir? (PAUSE) Oh? Incidentally ... Friday morning's Central Express has very few bookings... I've checked.

(WOOLCOT GLARES, THEN SMILES, AND SHAKES HIS HAND WARMLY)

(LIGHTS FADE)

(END OF SCENE)

ACT TWO   **SCENE NINE**

THE WOOLSHED AT YARRAHAPPINI FRIDAY – TWILIGHT

(SIGN ON PROSCENIUM ARCH READS, 'NEXT FRIDAY')

AT RISE:

THE WOOLSHED IS EMPTY, BUT SOON THE ENTIRE POPULATION OF "YARRAHAPPINI" STATION APPEARS: STATION HANDS, GIRLFRIENDS AND WIVES, MR AND MRS HASSAL CARRYING EXTRA KITCHEN BASKETS OF CUTLERY AND PLATES, ESTHER AND ALL THE CHILDREN, WITH JUDY IN CHARGE OF THE LITTLE GENERAL. THEY ARE ALL EXCITED AND SCRUBBED CLEAN AND DRESSED FOR THE BUSH DANCE)

MEG:

(SEEING LITTLE GRANDMA STRUGGLING WITH HER LOAD) Please let me carry some of that, little Grandma.

MRS HASSAL:

Yes, Meg. I think I will. I thought 'cook' may need some extra plates and cutlery, now that there are so many of us here from the homestead.

(PIP AND JUDY CATCH UP TO MEG AND THE HASSALS AS THEY ENTER THROUGH THE MASSIVE OPEN HIGH DOUBLE DOORS OF THE WOOLSHED. ON ENTERING, A CONVERSATION IS OVERHEARD, BUT NOT BY MR HASSAL AND ESTHER WHO MOVE IMMEDIATELY TOWARD A LARGE PODIUM ON WHICH THE BUSH BAND IS SETTING UP)

TETTAWONGA:

Marse Gillet b'in on the burst again!

WOMAN KITCHEN HAND:

'Lor! I'm not surprised. 'ee's b'in too sober late days to keep it up. S'pose he's been trying to last the visitor's out, but found it too much.

(MEG IS OF DEVASTATED ON OVERHEARING THIS)

MEG:

(TO MRS HASSAL) So that's where he's been these last three days. Drunk. I thought he was on business for Grandpa?

MRS HASSAL:

Don't judge too harshly, Meg. Sometimes things aren't quite the way they seem.

MEG:

(SHE IS ASHAMED) He's weak and ignoble.

(THE YOUNGER CHILDREN CATCH UP TO THEM)

BABY:

Ve haven't got our thom-a-hawks vif uth.

MRS HASSAL:

There aren't any bushrangers here, Baby.

BUNTY:

Anyway, I've got my catapult (HE TAKES IT OUT OF HIS POCKET)

PIP:

You'd better stay near Tettawonga, Baby. He's good with a tomahawk. He'll look after you.

NELL:

Don't mock.

BABY:

Yeth. Don't mock.

(THE WOOLCOT CHILDREN MOVE TO HELP THE MUSICIANS SET UP. JUDY TAKES THE GENERAL AND DEPOSITS HIM IN A VANTAGE POINT TO WATCH PROCEEDINGS))

JUDY:
(AS SHE PASSES MEG) Keep away from Mr Gillet.

MRS HASSAL:
(OVERHEARING) Things seem so black and white when you're young, don't they? As you get older you will find shades of grey form in between.

MEG:
(UNCONVINCED) Yes, Grandma.

MRS HASSAL:
(TO MEG) Go over and help set the tables. We're going to have fun tonight.

MEG:
(A SMILE RETURNS TO HER FACE AS HER MOOD CHANGES) Yes, we are.

PIP:
(WHISPERING TO MEG SO TO BE UNHEARD BY MRS HASSAL) Fizz is right about Mr Gillet. Sis knows best.

(A STATION-HAND TAKES THE BASKET FROM MRS HASSAL AND THEY MOVE OFF. MEG CARRIES A BASKET TO ANOTHER OF THE TABLES NEARBY WHERE SHE STARTS TO TAKE OUT UTENSILS. MR GILLET SUDDENLY APPEARS FROM NOWHERE MEG IS SHOCKED, DROPPING ALL SHE IS CARRYING)

MR GILLET:
(MOVING TO HELP HER) I will do this – you look hot, Miss Meg; sit down and let me do this.

MEG:

(VERY COLDLY AND NOT LOOKING AT HIM) Thank you, but I prefer to do it myself.

(SHE SETS THE CUTLERY AS HE WATCHES SADLY. FINALLY HE TAKES THE BLUE RIBBON FROM HIS POCKET AND MOVES TO GIVE IT TO HER)

MR GILLET:

I have to give you this again.

(HE HANDS HER THE BLUE RIBBON AND WITHOUT LIFTING HER EYES, SHE TAKES IT AND SLIPS IT INTO HER POCKET)

MR GILLET:

I had almost hoped you would say I might keep it, in spite of everything. Just as a comfort.... against the future, but your lips are too severe, Miss Meg, for me to cherish the hope any longer.

MEG:

It would be no use.

MR GILLET:

Ah well, I dare say you are right.

MEG:

Of course, if you really want the ribbon you can have it. (SHE TAKES IT AGAIN FROM HER POCKET)

(HE MAKES NO ATTEMPT TO TAKE IT)

MR GILLET:

(BECOMING UNPLEASANT) Keep it to tie your hair again, little girl, after all, I don't suppose it would be any use.

(THE WEATHER OUTSIDE HAS TURNED DARK AND BLUSTERY. IT BEGINS TO THUNDER AND RAIN. THE 'GENERAL' BECOMES FRIGHTENED. JUDY RUSHES TO COMFORT HIM)

JUDY:

Don't be scared, General... it's only a summer storm.

MR HASSAL:

Shouldn't last. Bit of weather about though.

MRS HASSAL:

(CUPPING HER HANDS) We need the rain... but not today, thank you so much, Lord.

(MR HASSAL SQEEZES ESTHER'S HAND AS HE MOUNTS THE PODIUM. HE LOOKS TO THE BAND. THE DRUMMER KICKS HIS TRASH CAN BASS DRUM AND BANGS HIS SAUCEPANS IN A CALL FOR SILENCE)

MR HASSAL:

(ADDRESSING ALL) Are.... we.... ready?

ALL:

We are!

CHILDREN:

Yeaah!

MR HASSAL:

Before we begin … I've a surprise for you … (TAKING ESTHER BY THE HAND) as if you didn't know....

(HE IS INTERRUPTED BY A SUDDEN COMMOTION AT THE WOOLSHED ENTRANCE. ALAN AND WOOLCOT, CLAD IN OIL-SKINS, HAVE ARRIVED. ESTHER SEES THEM FIRST, EXCUSING HERSELF URGENTLY FROM HER FATHER, SHE CLIMBS DOWN FROM THE PODIUM, THEN HESITATES, THEN HURRIES TO HER HUSBAND. MEG QUIETLY GRAVITATES TO ALAN, HANGING UP THE OILSKINS ON A PEG. JUDY MOVES TOWARD HER FATHER VERY CAUTIOUSLY, PAUSING, LEAVING THE GENERAL ON HIS VANTAGE POINT AND ON HIS OWN. WOOLCOT NOTICES JUDY'S APREHENSION.

WOOLCOT:

Judy …

JUDY:

(CAUTIOUSLY) Yes, father?

(WOOLCOT SLOWLY HOLDS OUT HIS HAND FOR JUDY TO SHAKE. SHE HESITATES, MOVES SLOWLY TOWARD HIM, THEN RUNS, GRABBING HIS HAND ENTHUSIASTICALLY, THEN JUMPS INTO HIS ARMS. HE GIVES HER A MIGHTY TWIRLING-AROUND HUG, HOLDING HER, THEN GENTLY PUTS HER DOWN. HIS ATTENTION TURNS LOVINGLY TOWARD ESTHER.

EVERYONE WATCHES AS WOOLCOT SLOWLY WALKS TO HER, BOWING VERY FORMALLY.

204

ESTHER CURTSIES FORMALLY. THERE IS A
PAUSE. A LONG, BREATHLESS SILENCE)

WOOLCOT:
Mrs Woolcot... if you do not have this dance with me, I
shall be very disappointed.

(ESTHER HOLDS OUT BOTH HANDS TO HIM. HE
TAKES THEM. THEY LOOK AT EACH OTHER, THEN
TO THE BAND WHO ARE READY TO PLAY.
SUDDENLY A MIGHTY CRACK OF THUNDER
SHAKES THEM ALL. A STAB OF LIGHTENING
FOLLOWS.

THE LITTLE GENERAL, SITTING ON HIS OWN IS
FRIGHTENED. HE WANDERS OFF.

NO-ONE IS AWARE THE GENERAL IS MISSING AS
THE RAIN INCREASES ON THE TIN ROOF AND
EVERYONE HUDDLES TOGETHER INSIDE THE
SHED.

SUDDENLY THERE IS A TREMENDOUS CRASH OF
THUNDER, AND A BOLT OF LIGHTENING.
EVERYONE IS STARTLED. JUDY LOOKS TO THE
GENERAL'S VANTAGE POINT, SEES IT IS EMPTY
THEN LOOKS AROUND)

MR HASSAL:
That was a bit close.

JUDY:
General? … General, where are you?

(OTHERS START TO LOOK AROUND. JUDY RUNS
TO THE DOOR AND LOOKS OUT. MR HASSAL TOO
HEADS TO THE DOOR, FOLLOWED BY SOME OF
THE OTHERS, JUST AS THE SKY TURNS BLACK
AND A DELUGE OF RAIN SMASHES DOWN ON THE
ROOF)

JUDY:

General? You come back here! General!!!

(JUDY DASHES OUTSIDE)

MR HASSAL:

Judy!! … You can't go out in that!

(MR HASSAL, WOOLCOT AND ALAN LEAD
SEVERAL STATIONHANDS OUT THE GREAT OPEN
DOORS INTO THE STORM BEHIND HER. PIP TRIES
TO JOIN BUT IS BLOCKED BY ESTHER)

ESTHER:

No, Pip. You stay here.

MRS HASSAL:

(LOOKING INTO THE DISTANCE) Where are they?

(THERE ARE MORE CATACLYSMIC CRACKS OF
THUNDER AND ZIG-ZAGS OF LIGHTENING. THE
RAIN BEGINS TO ABATE, THE THUNDER AND
LIGHTENING STOP, BUT THE SHREIK OF WIND
INCREASES IN INTENSITY)

PIP:

(LOOKING OUT) I can see Judy. Can't see The General....

ESTHER:

Yes... there he is! Near the billabong.... (POINTS) under the trees.

MRS HASSAL:

(ALARMED) Trees … ((SHOUTS)... keep away from the trees!

(A FREAK BOLT OF LIGHTENING HOLDS FOR A SECOND OR TWO OVER THE SCENE. MEG AND NELL SCREAM AS A SIMULTANEOUS CRACK OF THUNDER DROWNS OUT ANYTHING WE HAVE HEARD BEFORE)

ESTHER:

(HORRIFIED) Judy … ! No!!

(A FRIGHTENING YELLOW-RED LIGHT FILLS THE SKY. IN THE SUSPENDED LIGHT OF THE LIGHTENING WE SEE OUTLINES OF JUDY AND BEHIND HER, THE THREE ADULTS MOVING SLOW MOTION UNDER A HUGE TREE. ALL IN THE WOOLSHED WATCH AND GASP AUDIBLY.

ALMOST AS IF IT IS THE "EYE" OF THE STORM, THE WIND NOISE CEASES, AND WE HEAR VERY CLEARLY THE TEARING OF TIMBER, AND SEE IN THE DISTANCE THE SLOW TOPLING AND ENORMOUS CRASH OF THE TREE)

ESTHER:

Oh my God!

MEG:

(SCREAMS)

(MRS HASSAL SUPPORTS ESTHER WHO IS ABOUT
TO FAINT. MEG, NELL AND BABY HOLD EACH
OTHER IN A DESPARATE HUDDLE AS BUNTY
CRIES HIS EYES OUT ALONE. PIP RUNS OUTSIDE
NOW UNRESTRAINED AS THE OTHERS REACT.
THE RAIN HAS ALMOST STOPPED AND MORE
FOLK FOLLOW PIP. ALL SEEM AWARE OF GREAT
IMPENDING TROUBLE.

IN THE SHED ALL CROWD THE ENTRANCE,
LOOKING TOWARDS THE BILLABONG. THERE IS A
LONG WAIT IN SILENCE. IT IS LIKE A TABLEAU IN
A GREEK TRAGEDY.

THE CROWD PARTS AS WOOLCOT ENTERS,
CARRYING THE UNCONCIOUS FIGURE OF JUDY.
SHE IS RAINSOAKED AND DISHEVELLED. ALAN
AND MR HASSAL FOLLOW, MR HASSAL HAND IN
HAND WITH THE LITTLE GENERAL, WHO IS
UNHURT)

MRS HASSAL:

(ALMOST WHISPERS) What happened?

MR HASSAL:

Little General ran under the tree... when it started to fall …

PIP:

(INTERRUPTING) Judy pushed him clear and saved
him…

(MEG SPREA DS A COAT ON THE FLOOR.
WOOLCOT LAYS JUDY DOWN ON IT, WITH
ESTHER'S HELP. ALAN KNEELS TO CHECK HER
EYES AND FEEL HER PULSE.

THE OTHERS KEEP A DISTANCE BACK,
WATCHING IN SHOCKED SILENCE)

ESTHER:
Alan... will she be all right … ?

ALAN:
(ON CHECKING THE VITAL SIGNS HE IS
ALARMED) I … I can't say. (HE SHAKES HIS HEAD) I
don't think there's anything I can do. She needs real help. I
can't … not here... (LOOKING TO ESTHER ALMOST IN
TEARS) I'm so sorry. There's nothing I can do. Nothing …

(HE RISES. MEG COMFORTS HIM. THEY HOLD
EACH OTHER, EACH TRYING TO COMFORT THE
OTHER)

ESTHER:
Oh... please God …

WOOLCOT:
(BESIDE HER) Judy... Judy …

(WOOLCOT STROKES HER FACE. MRS HASSAL
INDICATES FOR THE CROWD TO MOVE BACK. IN
THE BACKGROUND THE SKY IS CLEARING, THE
STORM IS OVER AND A RAINBOW IS FORMING)

JUDY:
… Father … Hold my hand …

(HE TAKES HER HAND IN HIS)

WOOLCOT:
Judy... I'm here …

JUDY:
Won't finish it now …

WOOLCOT:
What?

JUDY:
My poem... it was going to be a surprise... won't finish it now …

WOOLCOT:
You will... of course you will …

JUDY:
No …

WOOLCOT:
Judy, I like your poems [A PAUSE ALARMED]... Judy?

JUDY:
... I'm a little bit frightened, Daddy …

WOOLCOT:
I'm here …
(WOOLCOT TAKES JUDY IN HIS ARMS)

(BUNTY GETS ON HIS KNEES, HANDS TOGETHER IN PRAYER)

BUNTY:
God... make her better.

JUDY:
Daddy …

WOOLCOT:
I'm here …

(WOOLCOT HOLDS HER CLOSER)

WOOLCOT:
Judy I... I think [AFTER A MOMENT] that
"Little children, when they die,
return to where they came from, in the sky,
and every child becomes a shining star,
God doesn't care how good or bad they are.
And in the evening, when Our Lord looks down,
the stars are all... all...

JUDY:
(SMILES)... the jewels in his crown."

(SUDDENLY JUDY HALF LIFTS HER HEAD,
LOOKING THROUGH THE DOORWAY OUTSIDE)

JUDY:
The sky … look at the sky … It's a rainbow day.

(HER HEAD FALLS BACK. WOOLCOT KISSES HER
ON THE FOREHEAD. HER HEAD TURNS SLOWLY
TO ONE SIDE AND WOOLCOT CALLS SUDDENLY)

WOOLCOT:
Judy, Judy, Judy!

(JUDY HAS SUCCUMBED)

WOOLCOT:
(A PAUSE AND HE TREMBLES IN SHOCK, A
BROKEN MAN) Ooooh....

(LIGHTS FADE QUIETLY)

(END OF SCENE)

ACT TWO   SCENE TEN

BARE STAGE – LIGHTS DIMMED

(IN SILENCE THE FOUR STAGE HANDS FROM THE
END OF ACT ONE [HEAD TO TOE IN OMINOUS
BLACK] MARCH OUT BACK STAGE PROMPT
DIAGONALLY IN A LINE TOWARD FRONT STAGE
OFF PROMPT, FORMING AS BEFORE INTO TWO
LINES OF TWO, THEN ABOUT TURN AND STAND
TO ATTENTION. TWO HORSE IMAGES LOWER
FROM THE GRID TO FALL OVER EACH OF THE
TWO LINES TURNING THEM INTO TWO HORSES
STANDING SIDE BY SIDE POINTING BACK
UPSTAGE FROM WHERE THEY HAVE COME. THE
SHAFTS BELONGING TO THE HEARSE WAITING IN
THE WINGS ARE PART OF THE HORSE CLADDING.
SFX - A WHIP CRACKS OFF STAGE. THE TWO
HORSES START A VERY SLOW FUNERALEAN CLIP
CLOP SIDE BY SIDE TOWARD THEIR
DESTINATION. THE HEARSE CONTAINING JUDY'S
WHITE COFFIN IS DRIVEN BY TWO FUNERAL
RAMROD-STRAIGHT GROOMSMEN, ONE OF
WHOM HOLDS THE REINS. ETHEL TURNER'S
FINAL WORDS BEGIN AS THE HEARSE COMES
INTO VIEW. VERY GRADUALLY THE SCRIM
LOWERS AS THE HEARSE MOVES AND
DISAPPEARS EVER SLOWLY INTO THE WINGS
BACK STAGE PROMPT SIDE)

ETHEL TURNER:

> (O.S.) There was a green space on a hill-top, near some gold-crowned wattle trees.
>
> This is where they left little Judy. It looked like a tiny church-yard in a children's country, or a green corner with a white picket fence, and one garden bed.
>
> On their last night, no-one cried; they held back their tears until they had closed the gate behind them, and left Judy alone on the quiet hill-top.
>
> Then they went home, to pick up the threads of their lives, and go on with the weaving that must be done, or hearts would break.
>
> (DURING THIS THE SCRIM IS SOFTLY LIT, REVEALING AN ILLUSTRATION OF JUDY'S GRAVE INSIDE THE TINY WHITE PICKET FENCE. A SMALL WHITE WOODEN CROSS RESTS ON A NEWLY DUG MOUND OF EARTH. THE IMAGE SLOWLY FADES TO DARKNESS)
>
> (END OF SCENE)

ACT TWO   SCENE ELEVEN

'YARRAHAPPINI' - THE WOOLSHED - ONE YEAR LATER - TWILIGHT.

> (SUDDENLY THERE IS AN EXPLOSION OF WHITE LIGHT AS A SIGN AT TOP OF PROSCENIUM ARCH ANNOUNCES "ONE YEAR LATER")

ALDITH:

(O.S.) Daaaaarlings! Daarlings!

(ALDITH, RIDICULOUSLY OVER-DRESSED FOR A
COUNTRY WEDDING, ENTERS FRONT OF SCRIM
AS IT SLOWLY RISES ON A WEDDING THAT IS
TAKING PLACE BEHIND. SHE WAVES ACROSS THE
CROWD TO HER FRIENDS ANDREW [BEST MAN]
AND BEATRICE WITH JAMES GRAHAM, IGNORING
THE OTHERS AND THE DIGNITY OF THE
OCCASION. THE GUESTS ALL GASP IN SHOCK,
TURNING TOWARD ALDITH AS SHE RUDELY
INTERRUPTS THE CEREMONY.

THE WOOL-SHED IS DECKED IN BRIGHT FLOWERS
AND WEDDING DECOR. MEG STANDS WITH ALAN.
NEXT TO MEG, BRIDESMAIDS NELL AND BABY
STAND. BEHIND THEM CARRYING MEG'S TRAIN IS
A MUCH TALLER GENERAL. ALAN'S BEST MAN
AND BROTHER, ANDREW STANDS ON ALAN'S
OTHER SIDE. NEXT TO HIM ARE GROOMSMEN PIP
AND BUNTY. THEY ALL ARE TURNED AT 45
DEGREES TO THE AUDIENCE AS THEY FACE THE
SAME JOVIAL VICAR FROM ACT ONE. INCLUDED
IN THE BRIDAL PARTY ARE ESTHER AND
WOOLCOT, NOW DRESSED AS A WEALTHY
COUNTRY SQUIRE WITH AKUBRA HAT, AND AT
THE HEAD OF THE GUESTS CROWDED IN BEHIND
STANDS COLONEL BRYANT IN FULL MILITARY
DRESS WITH MRS BRYANT.

ALDITH:

(WOBBLING ON HER HIGH HEELS, BUMPING AND
BANGING HER WAY THROUGH THE GUESTS TO
FINALLY REACH HER FRIENDS. SHE IS

214

OBNOXIOUS AND SPEAKS LOUDLY) These new high heels struck a rock and rolled to one side… taking my ankle with it. (TO THE OTHERS) So sorry, I'm late. Daaarlings. (HER LAST WORDS FADE OUT EMBARRASSINGLY AS SHE SUDDENLY NOTICES THE REACTION OF THE OTHER GUESTS)

(THERE IS A LOUD COUGH FROM THE VICAR)

VICAR:

(RESUMING THE SERVICE) Ahem. (A PAUSE AS DECORUM IS RE- ESTABLISHED) Who gives this woman to be married to this man?

WOOLCOT:

(PROUDLY STEPPING FORWARD AND THEN BACKWARD TO STAND WITH ESTHER) I do.

(SMILES ALL ROUND AS ESTHER SQUEEZES HIS HAND)

VICAR:

For as much as Alan and….(A JOVIAL SMILE AS HE LOOKS AT HER) … Margaret …

(MEG LOOKS ADORINGLY AT ALAN - ABSOLUTELY IN LOVE)

VICAR:

.... have consented together in holy wedlock…

(A COUGH IS HEARD FROM ALDITH)

VICAR:

I declare them … man and wife. Doctor Alan and Mrs Margaret Woolcot. For those whom God has joined together, let no man put asunder!

(THE GUESTS BREAK OUT INTO LOUD APPLAUSE AS THE VICAR USHERS THE BRIDAL PARTY TOWARD THE DESK OFF PROMPT FOR THE SIGNING OF THE REGISTER. THE PARTY NOW INCLUDES COLONEL BRYANT WHO ACCOMPANIES MRS HASSAL. MRS BRYANT REMAINS WITH THE OTHER GUESTS. THE WEATHER OUTSIDE HAS TURNED DARK AND BLUSTERY AND IT HAS STARTED TO RAIN LIGHTLY TO SFX)

ESTHER:

(TO BRYANT) Thank you so much for acting as a witness in my father's absence.

WOOLCOT:

(VERY MUCH NOW THE LORD OF THE MANOR) Yes, Philip. It is much appreciated. It hasn't been easy at all since Mr Hassal's passing.

BRYANT:

(VERY AWARE OF THE NEW CIRCUMSTANCES) Only too happy to oblige … John.

(DISTANT THUNDER SOUNDS)

BRYANT:

Storm's on its way … as usual …

ESTHER:

Never mind that.

(SHE KISSES AND HUGS THE BRIDE AND GROOM AS THE VICAR OPENS THE REGISTER, POINTING TO WHERE SIGNATURES NEED TO GO ON THE PAGE. WOOLCOT HUGS MEG AND ESTHER THEN ADDRESSES ALAN FORMALLY)

WOOLCOT:

Well, my boy … Our congratulations. May we wish you life-long happiness and prosperity.

ALAN:

You may, sir. And thank you for being so gracious.

WOOLCOT:

Think nothing of it, my boy.

ESTHER:

(JOINING AND MRS HASSAL GRAVITATE INTO THE CONVERSATION) If only one could be so sure? Things seem so black and white... when young. But as one gets older.... many shades of grey form in between.

MRS HASSAL:

Now, where … have I heard that before?

(AMONG THE GUESTS WE BECOME AWARE OF TETTAWONGA AND MR GILLET, DRESSED IN TAILS AND HOLDING A TOP HAT)

MR GILLET:

(TO TETTAWONGA)

... Oh that I was where I would be!
Then I would be where I am not;
But where I am I still must be,
And where I would be I cannot".

TETTAWONGA:

(TO MR GILLET) Won't be the same roun' 'ere ... no more.

(LIGHTS GENTLY FADE)

(CURTAIN)

THE END

FOR ALL ENQUIRIES CONTACT: ORiGiN™ Theatrical
PO BOX Q1235, QVB Post Office, Sydney, NSW, 1230, Australia
Phone: (61 2) 8514 5201 Fax: (61 2) 9299 2920
enquiries@originmusic.com.au   www.origintheatrical.com.au
Part of the ORiGiN™ Music Group
An Australian Independent Music Company